Layla and Majnun

~NIZAMI~

For a complete list of our publications

go to the back of this book

Layla and Majnun

~NIZAMI~

Translation and Introduction

Paul Smith

NEW HUMANITY BOOKS

BOOK HEAVEN
Booksellers & Publishers

NEW HUMANITY BOOKS

BOOK HEAVEN
(Booksellers & Publishers for over 40 years)
47 Main Road
Campbells Creek Victoria 3451
Australia

website: newhumanitybooksbookheaven.com

ISBN: 978-1500423933

Poetry/Middle East/History/Literature/Mysticism/
Persian Poetry/Sufism/Islam

Front cover Azerbaijani folk art

CONTENTS

Introduction...

The Life and Poetry of Nizami of Ganja.

INTRODUCTION

The Life and Poetry of Nizami of Ganja.

Chapter 1.

The Early Years.

Nizami, or Abu Mohammed Ilyas ibn Yusuf ibn Zaki Mu'ayyad, was born around 1140 at Ganja in the land of Arran, Transcausian Azerbaijan. His father Yusuf left him very early an orphan* and when he was well-advanced in years we hear the lament of the son still full of sorrow...

Early, like my grandfather, so departed my father,
Yusuf, son of Zaki Mu'ayyad, one like no other:
why should I contend with the dominion of Fate?
It's Fate... can I fight against the opinion of Fate?
Still remaining and never to die... is whose father?
I was born so I should swallow blood of my father!
When I saw him go to where his father also went

I tore away his image from heart's bleeding vent...

to whatever happens, bitter or sweet, I submitted:

forgetting myself... power of Destiny I admitted.

His mother Ra'iseh was the daughter of a Kurdish chieftain and the poet dedicates some verses in the same place, in which he records his great love and his yearnings and sorrow at her early passing...

My mother, of distinguished lineage... Kurdish:

my mother, like my father, before me did perish.

To whom can I make my sorrowing supplication

to bring her to me... to answer my lamentation?

She devoured grief that was beyond all measure,

and perished in a whirlpool no one could endure!

My cup of sorrow is far too full that I should be

swallowing it in a thousand draughts! Ah, me!

For this woe and suffering that seems endless...

what remedy is there for me, but forgetfulness?

These verses are the only memorials that Nizami has left of his relations with his parents, but they do allow us to see his love for them in a clear light and perceive the deep impression which the early death of his parents made upon him which contributed to form a steady kind of seriousness which accompanied him throughout his whole life... and to his inclination for a solitary existence, renouncing many earthly delights.

Of an uncle, Khajeh Hasan, he thinks exactly as of his parents, for he had stepped into a father's place towards the orphan. He says of him...

When my master, whom I always called Uncle,

ceased to be and he as my wing ceased to pull,

my mouth being full of that bitter lump of grief

almost stifled reed of my throat without relief...

and I'd reason to fear that the groans I uttered

like steel chain my voice would have suffocated.

How Nizami's youthful years were passed, we do not know; but we do know that he acquired many acquisitions of knowledge, of which his first work shows the proofs. The Sheikh Akhi Farrah Rihani is named by Daulet Shah as his teacher. Of the religious instruction which he received in Ganja we are able to produce more than mere conjectures. Kasvini, the author of the 'Cosmography', who flourished not long after him, gives the following sketch of it: "Ganja is a strong old city in Arran, one of the frontier districts of Islam, since it lies near Kurg, or Georgia. The city is rich in wealth and the abundance of its productions. Its inhabitants are adherents of the Sunni and traditional teaching... people of piety and followers of the religious prescriptions who allow no one to dwell in their city who is not of their doctrine and of their faith, in order that it may not be destroyed by being amongst them. Their principal occupation consists in the handling of arms and the use of warlike instruments, because they live on the borders and in the vicinity of the unbelievers." This information is indirectly confirmed by the somewhat ancient *Yakat,* that from Ganja "very learned men have come out," of whom he also mentions some by name. From this it is clearly seen how piety became a distinguishing feature in the character and writings of this poet, who on account of his natural gentleness lost much of its bitterness and intolerance... and in his intimate feeling always inclined towards Sufism.

---

* Note: It is a fascinating fact that Persia's other two great exponents of the *ghazal,* Sadi and Hafiz, lost their fathers at an early age and also went to live with uncles... in the case of Hafiz his uncle was named Sadi! See introductions to my translations of Sadi's *ghazals, Divan of Sadi: His Mystical Love Poetry,* New Humanity Books 2010 and my complete *Divan of Hafiz,* New Humanity Books 1986. Revised edition New Humanity Books2010.

Chapter 2.

The Treasury of Mysteries

The first step that Nizami made from the dry asceticism which he had adopted to a more mystical view of the world, he has painted for us in the introduction to his first work (other than *ghazals* and other short poems that have not come down to us) called 'The Treasury of Mysteries' or *Makhzan-al-Asrar*. From this it appears, that it was mainly the lack of vitality in the society into which his pious existence had brought him that eventually revolted him. But what weighed upon him still more was the inactivity to which this soul-deadening asceticism condemned him. This left no room for the free expression of his inner heart's fire; allowed no movement to the impulses of the spirit of poetry with which he was richly endowed. Every enjoyment of the outward world was forbidden to him by his companions... 'those robbers, the senses'. Then came an illumination. As others are sleeping he sits voiceless, pained by his inner torments and he gropes through his past life. With the insight that it ought not to go on as it has, comes also the recognition of the path into which he ought now to strike. We hear how in this decisive moment of his life he tells himself to be warned and instructed...

The spirit of solitude said in a voice so serene:

give a pledge that you will be able to redeem.

Why go on casting water on this pure flame?

Why let the wind be master of your domain?

Give fever-bringing dust to the funeral pyre;

to that ruby inside you give the glowing fire!

Don't shoot arrow if target's your own reason!

Use less whip when the racehorse is your own!

From now on you mustn't sit careless anymore:

if your heart is stubborn, batter down the door.

Under the wide dome of this fair blue canopy...

sing the story of your heart like a sweet melody.

Keep far from those highwaymen, those desires:

heart knows the way, listen to what it inspires!

A nature which submits to the guiding of reason,

will wait for ready money of a forty-year season;

better than it maturing for forty years... let it be

working for what is needed for its further journey.

Now you need a friend... so be deluded no longer:

do not keep on repeating a forty-year-old lecture...

take your arm from garment and look for help, go!

For heart's sorrow find that one who it does know!

Don't feed on grief while there is another grieving;

break the neck of grief by with a friend it sharing.

For that soul that's captured by trouble and strife,

Friend of friends is the powerful support of his life.

Though being a king is not something to be hated,

when I look, nothing than a friend is higher rated.

Nothing deserves to be preferred to being a friend,

a friend who will hold you by the hand to the end;

that friend... tightly by the cords of the heart tie:

your clay... mingle it with that one's water... try!

And now, what was before the repressed voice of his naturally cheerful disposition, broke forth with fresh strength. The one-sided direction given to it was broken and no longer was a gloomy inactivity to rob him of a wise enjoyment of this world. He surrendered himself in trust to the vivid emotions of his own heart, as he says himself...

A heart to which the Supreme Lord has spoken

becomes a union of body and soul... unbroken:

the universe is illuminated by the heart's star,

and the twins of the heart... form and spirit are.

When the shackles which had bound his inward freedom fell... also fell away the chains that had before restrained his poetical talent...

The riches of my heart made my tongue rich also,

my nature now full of joy, all its sorrows let go:

my cold tears now flowed from a hot fountain...

for heart made my pot boil over! Don't constrain!

Yet the separation from those who had been his companions before this momentous change in him was not altogether easy...

My fellow-travellers are inexperienced... I'm new to travelling;

bitterer is separation from friends than loneliness I'm knowing.

The 'Treasury of Mysteries,' *Makhzan-al-Asrar* was probably completed during 1171 when the poet was in his early thirties and is composed of 2260 couplets. It is the production of a poetical nature, which has not yet arrived at a full consciousness of its striving for perfection. Composed of twenty discourses each one with a story... its content is religious and ethical topics joining both the spiritual and practical. What Nizami had previously carried about within himself he wished now to express in words: the views and experiences which before had built up in himself were now to be communicated to the world and at the same time the burden which had weighed him down fell from his heart. His inclination towards the epic in the form of the *masnavi* (rhyming couplets), which at a later period stepped into the foreground, showed itself even here... and so his narratives form, as in Sadi's *Bustan* (Orchard), the accompaniment of these meditations which are filled with a genuine Sufi spirit. That ease in rhyming of which at a later period Nizami boasts, he had not yet acquired in this his first completed work. He says...

So long must I rest my head upon my knee,

before thread's end comes to fingers of me.

His great faith in *sokhan*, discourse or eloquent speech through the poetic forms... becomes so strong that he believes that poets are creative artists with almost divine roles and he states...

The first movement of the Pen created

the first letter of the Word ever stated.

When lifting curtain of non-existence...

the Word was what They did dispense.

Until the Word allowed heart to speak,

the soul's free self the clay didn't seek!

When the Pen began to move... then...

it opened eyes of world by Word again!

Without speech world's voice is finished:

much is said, but Word isn't diminished.

In love's language soul is speech, no less;

we are speech... these ruins our palaces.

Of the high nature of his art he was then very conscious and he gives an animated expression of his intuitive perception of its worth and seriousness...

The mystical word which is veiled in poetry...

is a shadow of that which is veiled in prophecy.

Before and behind all the ranks of grandeur fit,

prophecy stands first and poetry is behind it...

these neighbours are intimates of one Friend:

that one is the kernel and this one is the rind.

But the poet must know how to preserve his inner worth and he must not by flattery treat his art merely as a commodity only to be sold...

Dead as gold is he who only regarding money,

gives away for gold the minted medal, easily!

He who barters for gold words bright as the day

gets a stone... giving an illuminating ruby away.

Doubtlessly, that tribe thinking itself so learned

is as much lower as it esteems itself so exalted!

A head seeming encircled with a sultan's crown

may fatefully tomorrow feel it a bandage of iron;

and he who like quicksilver hasn't felt gold grief

remains pure silver... free from the prince's iron.

This severe criticism, as is shown especially in the first couplet, is directed against the countless poets of that time who, flocking around the thrones of the less and greater princes, resigned themselves and their art as a plaything to their princely whims. Especially was this the case in Nizami's century, which had produced the greatest eulogistic poet, Anvari. Nizami never knew how to submit to this; in spite of many an opportunity offered to him to bring his life into connection with princely courts and to make his principal theme the laudation of princes... as did most of the poets of his time. This lofty understanding and opinion of his art worked enduringly on his destiny by building up a wall between him and his fellow-artists and was the cause of arguments with many of them.

Yet it was in the spirit of the times that the poets should dedicate their works to monarchs while on the other hand princes deemed it an honour to be sung to by poets. When Nizami wrote his *Makhzan-as-Asrar* he had not yet come into connection with any royalty. Shirvan appears to have been as yet not quite independent and so he turned his looks towards the southern neighbouring lands where the powerful Atabeg, Fakhr-ud-din Bahram Shah, laid the foundation of the dynasty of the Atabegs of Azerbaijan. In the section of the introduction which contains the eulogy of the king and in that in which he lays his work at his feet, only the name of Fakhr-ud-din is mentioned in the following couplets...

> Guardian monarch and refuge of princes...
> lord of scimitar, lord of diadem, priceless,
> although wielding the rigorous sword you
> come taking all crowns and thrones too...
> like khalifs, you scatter your treasures also,
> bestowing diadems... upon thrones you go.
> The edge of your sword is above all crowns,
> from kings... shouldn't you receive tribute?
> In this azure revolving sphere... the quality
> of a man... are the measures of his dignity!

In whatever exaggeration Nizami may have indulged in his eulogy of Bahram Shah, his proud self-consciousness never deserts him, especially his overflowing and unbounded reverence for poetry... and so he says...

> Though many are standing around the throne
> bowing as suppliants for favour of that one...

all being superior to Nizami in point of rank,

he is one... but what are the others? Be frank!

I, having arrived at the halting place with them

will push on my journey a little ahead of them:

I have made of my words a sword of hard stone,

and I will lower heads... of those who follow me.

As was stated earlier, Nizami's first book contained mainly poetry in the *masnavi* form, with stories of mystical and moral teachings. The following tale about Jesus is a good example and is often quoted...

The Messiah's feet, which forever shows us the world,

into a small bazaar they journeyed one day where unfurled

before him a scene of a wolf-dog lying upon the road...

like Joseph leaving the well, its soul had left its load.

Over that dead body many sightseers stood and gaped,

hovering, vultures at carrion, mouths open they stared.

One finally said: "This is so disgusting to the brain

it wants to black out like a useless lamp: it's a pain!"

One held his nose, one shut her eyes and looked away

and amongst those standing there loud voices did say...

"A detestable creature!" "It defiles the earth and the air!"

"Its eyes are blurred!" "Its ears are filthy!" "Ribs are bare!"

Each one gathered there said something that was similar:

each one at the poor dead body threw abuse even crueler.

When the time came... it was Jesus' turn to say something,

not disturbing the surface he went straight to the meaning:

he said: "Inside His palace many engravings one can find,

but pearls as white as this wolf's teeth... ah, one of a kind!"

All gathered there, from hope and fear their teeth did bare...

whitened with oyster's burnt shell, over wolf's shell there!

The abusive crowd became silent and ashamed like one

rebuked by an insight and wisdom greater than their own.

There is never one of His creatures that so abused can be...

without something fine inside, that a loving eye can see.

Another example from Nizami's first book, in his group of five poetic *masnavi* masterpieces called the *Khamsa* or 'Quintet' (also called the *Panj Ganj* or 'Five Treasures')... the 'Treasury of Mysteries', tells the story of the famous monarch of Persia Nashirwan the Just (the son of Kobad, ascended the throne 531 and died 579 A.D.) and his education as to the misuse of power by his wise vizier...

Intent upon sport, Nashirwan on a particular day

spurred his horse on to quickly take him far away

from his retainers... it was only his trusted vizier

who rode out with him... no other soul was near.

Crossing a game-stocked plain he halts and scans

a ruined village, one of his enemy's devious plans.

Nearby there were sitting two owls, not far apart,

their dreary hooting chilled the monarch's heart.

"What secrets do they whisper?" Asked the king

of his advisor: "what means the song they sing?"

"O sovereign," the minister replied... "I now pray

you will forgive me for repeating what they say...

sound they make isn't a song or a calling to mate:

it is really the question of a betrothal they debate.

That bird gave her daughter to this one, and now

asks him for a proper portion as a dowry to allow

the union, saying: "This ruined village give to me,

and some others as well... perhaps two or three."

"Let it be," the other cries out... "our rulers leave

to pursue injustice again... and they don't grieve,

and if one worthy monarch should happen to live,

a hundred thousand ruined homes I would give."

Although not widely known in the west (though it should be because of G.H. Darab's admirable literal English translation published in 1945) the 'Treasury of Mysteries' is highly regarded in its homeland and was a strong influence on the following works by three other significant poets: Amir Khusrau: *Matla'-Anwar* or 'The Dawn of Lights'; Khaju Kermani: *Rowzat al-Anvar* or 'The Garden of Lights' and Jami's *Tuhfat al-Ahrar* or 'The Gift of the Noble'.

Chapter 3.

Khosrau and Shirin.

The powerful Atabeg, Bahram Shah a patron of poetry, appears to have paid attention to the homage of the poet, even though Nizami held himself aloof from the court, by rewarding him with 5000 dinars. But a greater treasure was soon to be given to him. The king of Darband had heard his work and out of gratitude sent him the beautiful Kipchak slave-girl Appaq (meaning 'snow white'). Nizami soon fell in love with her and they were married. They lived happily together for about six years when she tragically died leaving the poet with a little boy, Mohammad... the light of his eye, whom he often advised in his works that followed. Years later when he was about 57 years old and writing his last book, the second volume of the *Iskandar-nama* or 'Alexander Book'... *Khirad-nama* or 'Book of Wisdom', he would say of her...

Heaven, which to me was once benign...

gave me a bride who was likewise fine,

in the same way she loved, served me...

in thought, deed she served me perfectly.

A sweet rose, tinged as with my blood…

she knew no other than me in the world.

A fountain of light she was to this eye…

warding off evil eyes that on me did lie.

Destiny, that robber, took her too soon…

you might say "She was and was gone!"

For all kindness I received through her…

I pray for His kindness to come to her!

His second epic 'Khosrau and Shirin' of about 7000 couplets was composed during the years 1177-81 at the request of Seljuq Shah Tughril the Second who had invited him to write a love story "paint a *new* image for the world"… although taking and expanding on the Sasanian royal romance first encountered in Firdousi's epic… *Shah-nama,* the tragic portrait of Shirin would be drawn from his beloved Appaq.

In this work Nizami says about this change from the religious *masnavi* to the romantic…

Treasure like 'Makhzan-al-Asrar' being mine,

why then should I now to a romance incline?

Yet… in the world there is no one that today

who passion of romance does not hold sway.

He writes the perfect portrait of Shirin as the ideal woman... beautiful, pure, brave, devoted and wise. His relationships with his future wives would help him to portray other feminine heroes in a way that had yet to be perceived in the world's literature and become a major component in the uniqueness of his creations. Nizami's profound knowledge of astronomy, mathematics, medicine, jurisprudence, philosophy, music and the arts shines through in this work as it does in those that follow.

Some of 'Khosrau and Shirin' relates the triangular love story of Khosrau, king of Persia and his princess Shirin and Farhad an eminent sculptor. Farhad's passionate love for the same woman worried the monarch. To remove him from his court the king required him to cut a channel for a river through the mountain of Behistun near Kirmanshah, and to decorate it with sculpture. He promised that if Farhad should accomplish this stupendous task... he would receive as his bride the object of his love... the beautiful Shirin! The love-crazed artist accepted the work on that condition. It is related that as he struck the rock, he constantly invoked the name of Shirin...

On that lofty slope of Behistun... the lingering sun
looks down on his ceaseless work, long ago begun;
the mountain now trembles to the echoing sound

of the falling rocks that from both sides rebound.
Each day, all respite and all repose are self-denied,
without a pause the thundering strokes are plied;
the mist of night around the summit softly coils,
but still Farhad, the lover-artist... toils and toils!
As always... the flash of his axe as he cuts again,
and he sighs into the wind, "Ah, no... no Shirin!"
A hundred arms are weak to even one block move
out of the thousands moulded by the hand of love
into fantastic shapes and forms of amazing grace,
crowding each spare space of that majestic place.
The rock-piles give way and the high peaks divide,
and the stream comes gushing on, a foaming tide:
a mighty work that for many an age will remain...
the result of his great love, passion... and his pain.
While flows that milky flood from Allah's throne,
and rushes as a torrent from that yielding stone.
Sculptured nearby, a stern Khosrau does stand...
and frowning, sees obeyed his harsh command...
while she... the fair beloved, from being his wife
awakes from glowing marble... into another's life.
O unfortunate young man! O toil repaid by woe!

A king as your rival... and the world as your foe!

Will she... wealth, splendor, pomp, for you leave,

and in the genius, truth and love of you... believe?

Around the royal pair, see: chiseled courtiers wait,

and slaves and pages grouped in a solemn state;

from columns, carved wreaths of garlands grow,

below fretted roofs... where stars appear to glow:

fresh leaves and blossoms spring up everywhere,

feathered throngs their love sing here and there.

Angels' hands might have created those stems...

where the dew-drops hang their fragile diadems,

and strings of pearl... sharp-cut diamonds shine,

new from the caves... or, recently from the mine.

"Ah, no... Shirin!" At every stroke he sadly cries:

with every chiseling stroke... fresh miracles arise.

"For you my whole life one ceaseless toil has been,

but now inspire my soul again! Ah, now... Shirin!"

Years later Farhad achieved his stupendous task, and with such exquisite skill that the greatest sculptors from all over the world came to see his work and were astonished and confounded at the genius of this love-intoxicated soul. Farhad was pausing, weary, at the completion of his work, with his chiseling axe in his hand, when his rival (having heard he had completed the work that he thought was impossible) so that he wouldn't have to give up Shirin to him... devised a terrible trick. Khosrau sent an old woman Farhad would trust with the false message that Shirin was dead...

He heard the fatal news... with no word, no groan;

he neither spoke nor moved... transfixed to stone.

And then, with a frenzied start, he raised up high

his arms, wildly throwing them towards the sky;

he then heaved so deep a sigh that you would say

that a spear into his poor heart had found its way.

"Ah no... all my labour!" This was his bitter cry...

"With my reward still not won, in grief now I die!

O no... all this wasted labour that took my youth!

Ah, no! Hope became hopeless... that's the truth!

I tunneled the mountain's walls: now see my prize!

My work is wasted... here, the true hardship lies!

I, just like some kind of fool the red rubies coveted:

see... now worthless pebbles fill my hands instead!

What fire is this... that me, does totally consume?

What flood is it which now hurls me to my doom?

The world is without both sun and moon for me...

my garden lacks its box-tree, also its willow-tree.

For the very last time my beacon-light has shone;
not Shirin... but the sun from me has really gone!
O no... now weep for such a sun and such a moon,
which a black eclipse has swallowed all too soon!
Before this, the wolf would pass a hundred sheep,
but now... on the poor man's lamb it's sure to leap.
Over my sad heart the fowls and the fishes weep,
for my life's stream into the darkness does creep.
Why have I been parted from my beloved so dear?
Now that Shirin is gone, why should I stay here:
without her face should I desire to live, to thrive?
It would serve me right if I were to be buried alive!
Fallen to the dust, my cypress lies down... dead:
shall I still remain to throw dust onto my head?
My smiling rose has now fallen from off the tree:
the garden is nothing but some prison now to me.
My bird of Spring has from the meadows flown...
and I, like the thunder-cloud, will weep and groan.
My world-enkindling lamp has gone out for ever...
will not my day be turned to night today, forever?
My lamp has gone out and coldly blows the gale...
my moon is now dark and my sun has gone pale.

Beyond the portals of death... my Shirin I'll greet,

so with one leap... death, I now hasten to meet!"

Far into the wide expanse his chisel-axe he flung,

and from that terrible precipice at once he sprung.

The rocks, the sculptured caves, the valleys green,

sent back unheard his dying cry: "O, no... Shirin!"

Some time after he had finished the book and had received nothing from Shah Tughril the Second who had recently passed away, his brother Shah Kizil Arslan who was impressed by Nizami's masterpiece that in its sincerity is unequalled in Persian literature, invited him to his court and for probably the first and last time Nizami accepted a royal request for his presence. When he appeared at court the new king was holding a party and after a distribution of honours and presents...

When they told him... "Nizami has arrived,"

banquet's joy to a triumphant pitch it sped.

He, looking respectfully upon my devotion,

not merely on woolly cap of a 'companion',

ordered wine to be removed from the party

and shut up tongue of the pipe immediately.

The reception was extremely gracious. The shah embraced the poet, asked him to take a seat and entered into close conversation with him in which Nizami didn't fail to display his full eloquence...

At one time I drew down tears as from a cloud...

then I made their joy smile like a rose, so proud.

He bestowed on Nizami a village and royal robes of honour and money... although the poverty of the village would eventually cause him to be ridiculed. Some years later Nizami was to wed again, this time to an unnamed princess!

Although other great writers such as Amir Khusrau, Salman and Jami have attempted this epic in verse none can compare with the beauty and honesty of this Nizami masterpiece. Although translated into French and German that there has not been an English translation is unfortunate and one hopes it will soon be rectified.

Chapter 4.

Layla and Majnun.

Seven years later in 1188 Nizami is found to be in a much happier frame of mind. One day he received a message, which gave him the opportunity of setting to work this new energy of his spirit. The king of neighbouring Shirvan, Abu 'l-Muzzaffar Shirvanshah Akhsitan, wished him to elaborate the love-story of the celebrated pair of young Arabian lovers Layla and Majnun. This king's origin, with whom began a new dynasty for Shirvan, reached back to the old kingly dynasties of Persia and so he regarded himself as *the* representative of Persian nationality and spirit and wished at least to animate his not very widespread dominion... by making it the protector of Persian literature. The request of the prince to Nizami had probably no other ground than to draw to his court from his quiet seclusion the poet who was already so renowned that he was able to say of himself...

I have brought to such refinement my enchanting poetry,

my name "The mirror of the world to come" will now be!

The task asked of him by no means at first appealed to Nizami. The subject proposed was indeed a worthy one... as he expressed himself about it...

Love stories... there are more than a thousand,

which by tip of a pen are made into a legend...

however this one is the king of all love-stories:

what can it be, with all artistry that in me lies?

But soon the subject appears to Nizami to be too dry to be turned into a great poem. The desolate Arabian wilderness for his theatre, two simple children of the desert as his heroes, nothing but an unhappy passion... this might well daunt even the poet of 'Khosrau and Shirin', which in everything, place, persons, and treatment, presented the greatest variety and grandeur. He says...

The entrance court of the story is too contracted:

poem would suffer, going backward and forward!

Race-ground of poetry ought to be more spacious

if it's to show off the ability of the rider, I stress.

A verse of Koran may deserve to be well known...

but, a commentary on it may become overblown.

Fascinations of poetry are its joys and flatteries;

from these two sources is derived its harmonies.

On such a journey in which I know not the way,

can I know where are the pleasant spots to stay?

There may be neither gardens nor royal banquets,

nor music, nor wine... not anything, but regrets.

Only rugged mountains and endless arid sands...

until poetry becomes an aversion in one's hands.

But the persuasion of his son Mohammad, at that time fourteen years old and his regard to the prince's request convinced him to overcome his reluctance and he soon began work. Nizami once aroused was able to exhibit an extraordinary activity. Within a short time he completed this master-work of love-poetry, which in the comprehensive laying-out of the plan and the connected execution of the several parts has remained unsurpassed although even such poets as Hatifi and Jami and the great Azerbaijani poet Fuzuli and many others inspired by Nizami's most famous work have at later periods treated the same subject. As to the quickness of the composition, Nizami says...

These four thousand couplets and some more

I wrote in less than months numbering four:

if I'd not been held up by another occupation,

fourteen nights may have seen its completion.

How was it possible for Nizami to complete this amazing literary masterpiece in such a short time? First he would have had access to the Arabic work of Abulfaraj al-Isfahani (died. 967), the *Kitab al-Aghani,* in which there is a chapter of over ninety pages on the young poet Qays or Majnun ('madman'), the lover of Layla who lived in the second half of the seventh century among the Bani Amir tribe in the Najd desert... a collection of traditions interwoven with verse. Other books earlier contained stories about the young lovers but Nizami's greatest source must have come from the collected poems of Qays Ibn Mulawwah (Majnun) himself (664-688 A.D.). What follows are some of my versions of his beautiful, powerful and haunting couplets or *qit'as* (fragments) from my translation of his poems: 'Poems of Majnun' New Humanity Books, 2012.

By these walls, these walls of Layla I'm passing
and now I'm kissing this wall, this wall Layla...
it's not Love of that house that's taken my heart
but of that one who dwells in that house, Layla!

I dream that I see us... two gazelles grazing;
in remote places, like meadows of h'awdhân.
I dream that I see us in the desert: two doves
flying to our nest,,, as the night come down.

As two fish in the sea I dream and think we

see when the Sea lulls us, as evening began.

I dream I see us… my life, your life together!

I see, I dream… even death, unites us again

on the bed of the tomb… lying side by side.

Retreat from the world, O falls well hidden!

We shall see, when resurrected, a new life…

universe as one, meeting, in the eternal plan.

When she was still an innocent girl my love for Layla started:

her growing breasts not noticed by those of her age, or clan.

And when we were children we took the animals out together…

if only we had like those animals, to grow up had never began.

The Amirite, Layla, sways back and forth on the camel's back…

those long curls with a silken ribbon she has tied together.

When on the top of her hair… her comb moves her dark curls,

from them fragrance of pink amber and sweet basil does scatter.

Pure white, shining like moon in night of whitest frost:

a true beauty to see, but, always beauty's cost is envy.

Crystal tears keep on reflecting black pupils brilliance;

in darkness, compared to them, antimony one can't see.
She is such a good girl that if one become too talkative
she becomes shy... and when speaking... speaks briefly.

This heart of mine feels like it's clutched in the tightening
talons of some bird, whenever that name of 'Layla'... I hear.
It's like ends of earth are a ring's band impressing me and
no space in length, breadth, width, depth to exist, can I bear!

My passion for Layla with more of Layla I have treated:
as a drunkard takes more wine to treat in his head, pain.
Can it be possible that Layla believes that I don't love her?
I do: 'By the ten days, and the even and uneven,'... again!*
*Note: Koran lxxxix, 2-3.

Wrapped in their cowls, through the night the pilgrims
in Mecca call out to God to forgive the sins they recite.
I called, "God, all I want is Layla, that will satisfy me!
If given her, I'll Your great repenter with all my might!"

See... when I am reciting the ritual prayers day and night
I face where she is, even if behind me is the place to pray!

But, I don't believe in more than one God: my love for her
is a choking, closing of throat, no doctor can cure any day.
I pray... but when I am remembering her I do not know if
I've at morning, twice, eight times faced her way, to pray.
I have not gone to her to be cured through looking at her...
I look at her, leave worse than before... no cure, does stay.

They told to me this: "If you wanted to... you could help
elsewhere find" and I answered, "No, please don't start!
The love I have for her has taken possession of my heart,
even if it is held back, it is forever... it will never depart!"

O heart of mine, you may die in sorrow... but, fear not...
that one who among men does fear, Eternity is not there.
You are in love with a girl that if given, you've Paradise:
try finding a way to where it's impossible to... get there.
I love Najd, of ever returning there I despair, each night.
No Layla, no Najd! Until Resurrection takes me, there!

The water that someone else offers might be sweet and
thirst may be quenched if I wanted, but, it I don't try!

All the passion of my love is dedicated only to that one,

though I'm certain my fate by her refusal will be to die.

I know I will be eventually killed by again lapsing into love,

but such relapses in the beginning were for me the only gain.

I'm given blows that will kill me because of my desperation:

Hope smiles in such a way, I'll continue through this pain.

Remembering her wears away my flesh... bones go,

like a knife carving away at wood to an arrow make!

It amazes me the story of 'Urwa the 'Udhrite's told

tribe to tribe... he died peacefully: death daily I take!

She asked me, "Why, why insane have you become?"

I answered her, "Love is worse than an insane brain!"

The one who truly loves... that one never gets over it,

while madman is raving only when he has fit. Insane!

I believe that this passion... this love that for her I have

will drive me to the wilds: no goods, no mother or father;

without one to turn to, to give a last will and testament,

with only horse and saddle as friends, my lament to hear.

All previous loves I had, by my love for her are eclipse…
and it is now more important than all… that went before.

That one is an unhappy one who in the evening is robbed
of his reason, and goes completely insane in the morning.
I am abandoned by my friends, except for those that say
that I'm mad and those who laugh, but away are staying.
When again I hear Layla's name then I know once again,
and… a new strength again into my sick brain is coming.

I keep trying to go to sleep but to me sleep won't come
because I'm hoping that a vision of your face I will see!
When I meet intending to talk about you… I run away,
so I can be alone and in secret I can my feelings display.

When I come it's not to words about another listen:
for other than you I've no interest, not in any other.
I look at who questions me, he thinks I understand:
but inside my mind is only you, he does not matter.

O dove of the forest… why, why do you continue to cry?
Is the one you love far off or to torment you is she trying?

When you are singing happily at morning on the branch,

is it passion and desire, that are cause... of your singing?

O you gazelles of her encampment where have you gone

with my Layla, when all stars in the sky have appeared?

The camp of Layla is at al-Mathaba, and around it birds

moan, cry and coo for outside her tent is always deserted.

My heart beats painfully with love and desire to see her:

how can this youthful passion of mine be ever appeased?

Shouldn't I follow Layla immediately to where she went:

to where she pitched her tent? People meet... are parted!

And... if this body of mine is lying far away from yours,

then in truth... Fate, my heart to yours, has been joined.

I'm a stranger in love, full of longing outside your tent...

outside a strange dwelling every one feels down- hearted.

Once again Destiny has dealt a heavy blow to my heart:

once again... this victim, by her lack of constancy is led.

O my Layla, it was only ever your glances satisfying me!

Only one who is satisfied by glances knows love, it's said!

Look at me! I go and go to sleep in the middle of the road,

like an owl's brother... whose wings have been fractured.

From their riverbed the torrents came rushing down…

from my eyes a great flow of tears they were drawing;

because I am knowing that to a far place their waters

are going, to a valley… its way to your feet, winding.

Now, they're bitter as they are passing; going to you

they flow and become sweet, with your scent playing.

When I am walking among my kinfolk, I am alone…

they are avoiding me but strangers they're welcoming.

If one is travelling to the south of Hima there is a hill

that stands there that I love, but near I'm never going.

What is worth of a world where one's love is far off…

and not one is getting up to you home be welcoming?

In his outward circumstances, Nizami's new work led to no change. The invitation from Shirvan could not move him to expose himself to the disagreeable atmosphere of the court. He however used the opportunity to warn himself and others…

Refrain from seeking the society of kings:

like exposing dry cotton to fire's burnings!

Light from the fire may be pleasant enough,

but to be safe one must stay a distance off:

moth that's allured by the flame of a candle

is burnt when a companion at banquet table.

Kizil Arslan's gifts had enabled him to live a quiet country-life. One can discover, among many personal intimations in the introduction to 'Layla and Majnun' that takes up over half the book, no complaint of want and even in the dedication appears no request alluding to it. Tranquilized by his quiet life, he says...

In your village, upon your own private estate,

do not think of eating from the other's plate.

Fortune will turn upon that unthinking fellow

whose foot beyond his garment he will allow.

That bird which flies beyond its own sphere...

measures its own flight with death's measure.

That serpent that's not keeping to its own path

twists itself in its twistings into its own death.

If the fox should begin to fight with the lion...

you know which hand the sword's lying upon.

But what he declines for himself he was not unwilling to grant to his son, who begs his father to permit him to go to the court of Shirvan and reside there as the companion of the young monarch. Nizami consents to this and it seems he sent his son as the bearer of the poem, for in his congratulation to the young monarch to whom he had already given information of his son's request, he says...

No doubt, you'll read the book of the Khosrus,

no doubt you'll study the sayings of the wise;

the treasures also hidden within this volume...

look upon in fullness of her circuit as the moon.

If you don't behold the face of this work's father,

please give your care to him... who is its brother.

Even out of this consent it is understood that Nizami would have wished to give another direction to his son's career than he had found for himself. He gives him practical counsels in the school of life. "If you also," he says to him, "have a talent for poetry, don't devote yourself to it... for that which pleases you soon becomes the most untrue." This judgment certainly does not apply to poetry as he himself understood it, for according to him... Truth is the very theme of poetry; but he means to warn his young son against that fake poetry which had spread itself through the courts of kings and filled him with a genuine abhorrence... and to the ensnaring atmosphere of which his son was about to be exposed. Then he says...

Although some poetry be of high dignity...

look for knowledge that is of some utility.

The Prophet said: "The science of sciences

is science of matter and of faith." You see?

In the navel of each there's a fragrant smell,

in the law and in medicine... this, you I tell.

But let the law instruct you in God's service,

let it not teach you how to lie... this, I stress.

If you are adept in both... with commonsense

you'll have reached the summit of excellence.

It is impossible to underestimate the effect of Nizami's 'Layla and Majnun' on the world over the past 800 years. Many poets throughout this period have copied or been influenced by his story of the young lovers. Many Master-Poets besides Attar, Rumi, Sadi, Hafiz and Jami have quoted from him or like him have used the story of the desperate lovers to illustrate how human love can be transformed into divine love through separation and longing. Paintings by the thousands, songs (even 'modern' ones by singer-songwriters such as Eric Clapton) in the many hundreds have been inspired by Nizami's long poem... also plays (Shauqi's is wonderful), operas, symphonies and films. Today the influence of his book seems more alive than ever and is growing. Shakespeare's 'Romeo and Juliet' is said to have been written under Nizami's influence (see bibliography).

The contemporary of Nizami Farid al-Din Attar (1142-1220) in his masterpiece long *masnavi poem Ilahi-nama*, 'Book of God, that was to influence Jalal-al-Din Rumi (1207-73) in the composing of his six book masterpiece *Masnavi*... tells a number of stories about the lovers to illustrate spiritual points...

There was a dervish who asked Majnun, "How old are you?"

That mad one replied... "A thousand and forty years is true!"

Dervish: "What's that, stupid? You're getting crazier, dummy?"

Majnun: "One supreme moment Layla showed her face to me...

I've lived a worthless forty years but worth a thousand years.

Being by myself those years I was poor in life's coin those years.

But... that one supreme moment, to a thousand years was equal

for in being with Layla time beyond measure into my life fell."

In his *Masnavi* Rumi tells of a conversation between the Caliph and Layla...

The Caliph said to Layla... "Are you really that one who

Majnun became lost and went mad over? That, is... you?

More beautiful than any other beauties... you... are not!"

She replied: "Quiet! Majnun, this one sees... you are not!"

And of the many mentions of Majnun (and Layla) scattered throughout the hundreds of *ghazals* in the *Divan of Sadi* this couplet is one of the most memorable...

O Sadi, in the opinion of lovers it is all the people

who are insane, while Majnun sane from birth is!

Iran's and perhaps the world's greatest mystical-love poet Hafiz of Shiraz (1320-1390) in his 'Book of the Winebringer' *masnavi* poem, obviously influenced by the one that begins and ends Nizami's 'Layla and Majnun', says...

In wisdom's opinion there's no better adorner of poetry

in this old sphere, than the pearls of speech of Nizami.

My version does not contain the long introduction but is the most complete in the English language and keeps to the correct rhyme-structure.

Chapter 5.

The Seven Portraits

Sometime after completing 'Layla and Majnun' tragedy struck again at the family life of the now famous poet with his second wife passing away prematurely. With his beloved son at court he was now alone again. But that did not stop him eventually beginning work on a new epic poem... *Haft Paykar* or 'The Seven Portraits' another long *masnavi* poem of over 5000 couplets.

In spite of the seclusion from the world to which Nizami condemned himself, he had to encounter many attacks. The poets of the royal courts looked unkindly at this consistent man, who, although disdaining to mingle with that group of poetical syco-phants, outshone them all in genuine glory. On the other side, again the precious treasures of poetry that he had already in store were exposed to these plagiarists who not only decked themselves out at the cost of our poet but also criticized him. But Nizami through the gentleness of his character had before been mainly silent; but now when he was about to step before the public again as he took up the pen he could not stop himself under the circumstances, from dedicating a special section to these unworthy fellow-poets. After challenging himself to break at last his long silence, Nizami paints the lofty powers of his poetic eloquence and then launches out against his assailants in the following terms...

These saltless scribblers... these eaters of bread

who live on the world under shade of my head!

To be slaying the game is the lion's business...

business of fox is to glut itself with the carcass:

it's better they feed on me, mouthful and gullet,

than that I should feed on others... and fat get!

Especially bitter is he against one who had made it his life's task to persecute him, partly with calumnies, partly with plagiarisms. With regard to the thefts that were made upon his poetry, it particularly upset him that these thefts should be so publicly shown about with impunity. But he calls to mind the inexhaustible well of his poetical gifts and says proudly...

In my lap the treasures of both worlds I hold...

why the thefts of those poor should I behold?

I'm bound to be upright to those in a deep pit,

whether they take what they want, or steal it.

Then alluding to the numerical value of his name, he describes his poetry as well guarded and secure from all inroads. Then he states that "pious and glorious men," of whom he mentions some from Adam to Mohammed, "have ever been obliged to "endure enmities without deserving them." He will never let himself to be hurried to return the wrong that has been done to him...

> For as long as I have lived, never in a violent
> way has the wing of a fly by me been bent...
> never mixed dregs in another's fresh water,
> sought to disturb another's condition, never!
> I've been endowed with gentle disposition...
> so a dog's faith I'd not try to bring undone.
> He who let me to dog give a lion's generosity,
> a lion's courage He has also bestowed on me.
> But I know it's better to conceal one's anger,
> and what has been said left unsaid is better.
> A one experienced in this world's commerce
> knows life isn't without jealousy or worse...
> and one intimately acquainted with our city,
> that one understands well my wares' quality:
> if he stretches out his hand with evil intent,
> I'm not his enemy, he is like a stranger, sent.

Keep silent, O heart, from all talking in vain,

eat your troubles with a cheerful face... again.

The *Haft Paykar* was dedicated to Ala' al-Din Korp Arslan the ruler of Maragha... who gave the poet full rein as to its subject matter and of this Nizami states...

I looked in the records of interesting histories...

for anything to help expand heart's boundaries:

from all that the Book of Kings was containing

I chose what was good in book to be combining.

In the first place I thought out a plan, ingenious,

and then embodied it in numbers... harmonious.

Where particles remained of this ruby-chipping,

of every atom I contrived to make something...

from those small fragments, like skilful jeweler,

I formed and polished a not worthless treasure...

so that the great, who know how to distinguish,

to choose from the portraits if it was their wish.

What the Book of Kings half-said I said fully:

what jewel he'd half-pierced I pierced wholly.

Whatever I perceived to be right and perfect,

not to disturb, as it stood at first, I did elect.

I made every effort that in the proper setting

to encase each choice and rare fragmenting.

Again, I searched books through the world...

for what had been hidden, almost forgotten;

whatever was written in Arabic and Persian,

tales preserved by Tabari and Bokhari's pen

and words through other volumes scattered,

and each pearl in a subtle fashion I arranged.

As to the application of the number seven, which in this work especially plays a considerable part Nizami says...

Portraits of this book, like those of the Magians,

I've portrayed after seven brides in bridal gowns,

so the seven brides which adorn the starry vault

will look with favour on my brides, find no fault:

and... in clothes like mine and as fellow-helpers

may drop down on each... as kindly benefactors.

But he guards himself against objections of lack of unity, and he always intends, as the painter would... however numerous the figures his picture may contain, to observe the necessary symmetry in the arrangement. Nor is he willing to be considered as a mere compiler... the work is written so as to be a special testimony to his spirit. The material worked upon becomes like the rainwater, which the oyster renders back as a splendid pearl. In every way it must be admitted that the direction which Nizami had always followed, that of elaborating the subjects of the old legends, has reached in the *Haft Paykar* its highest point... while Nizami in his love for the content has given an inward unity to this new work. That he did this with full knowledge is shown by the following couplets in which he states his relation to the other poets of his time...

Of that crowd which has preceded me,

no one made fresh fruit more than me.

If I've been wanting in using my store,

yet of the full meaning I've much more.

Shells, no kernels... like rain they all fell:

they answer me, "Kernel without shell!"

For all their precious poems so very new,

I'll not turn face from the old... the true!

'The Seven Portraits', *Haft Paykar,* Nizami's most Sufistic, complicated and ambitious mystical poem, tells of another Sasanian king, Bahram Gur and his guidance through the gross, subtle and mental worlds until he becomes the embodiment of the ideal king or Perfect Man, who after passing through feats physical in the first part... then through a symbolic visitation of seven princesses (seven planes in the involution of consciousness... as later portrayed by Attar in his 'Conference of the Birds' and explained more recently in great detail by Meher Baba in his book 'God Speaks'... see bibliography) in the second part, finally has to regain control of the kingdom (Unity) in the third part.

An interesting episode, illustrating the proverb that 'practice makes perfect,' occurs in this long poem. Bahram Gur, it is said had a favourite slave-girl named Fitna (meaning 'mischief') whom he would take with him on his hunting expeditions, where she would woo him during the intervals of rest with the strains of the harp in which she was skilled. One day the king had displayed his prowess in the chase and in archery to the utmost and expecting to win from his favourite some expression of admiration and wonder; but...

The slave-girl, prompted by a whim of willfulness,
admiration for his skillfulness refused to express.
The king was being patient, until a wild ass broke
out from its lair, then in this way to her he spoke:
"My skill, O my Chinese maid, your narrow eyes
cannot see, or on seeing, my skill you do despise.
My skill, which knows neither boundary nor end,
does not enter your narrow eyes, my blind friend!

See this beast... tell me to use my skill to impale

whatever spot you wish between head and tail."

"Please," she said... "your skill to me make clear:

with just one arrow... attach its hoof to its ear!"

The king, when this hard test was offered to him,

was prepared to gratify, to cure her willful whim;

he called for a crossbow, then quickly he did lay

within the groove for the shaft a hard ball of clay.

Straight into that quarry's ear the hard pellet shot,

instantly... the beast, to soothe the smarting spot,

and to remove that pellet of clay, its foot up high

it did raise, and then the king immediately let fly

an arrow like a flash of lightning which then sped

straight to hoof... nailing it to its ear on its head.

Then turning, to the maid of China said the king:

"Success! What now do you think of this thing?"

"For a long time... you this art have been taught,

a trick long practiced, to succeed in... is naught!

What a man has studied long, he does with ease,

and he solves the hardest problems, if he please.

That like this my lord the quarry's hoof should hit

doesn't prove skill, but 'practice makes perfect'."

The king, infuriated at his favourite Fitna's impertinence, gave her to one of his officers to be executed. She, by her pleading and assurances that her royal lover would repent of his hasty action, talked the officer into sparing her life and to conceal her in his hunting-lodge in the country. In this lodge was a staircase of sixty steps and Fitna, determined to prove the truth of her assertion that 'practice makes perfect,' obtained a new-born calf, and every day carried it on her shoulders up and down these stairs, her strength increasing as it grew. After six years her host, the officer, entertained Bahram Gur in this country-house and Fitna… veiling her face… seized the opportunity of displaying her accomplishment to her former lover by carrying the fully-grown oxen up and down the stairs. He was filled with admiration at this athletic feat and demanding to see her face, recognized with joy and forgiveness his sweetheart whom he had thought was dead.

Chapter 6.

The Alexander Books

With advancing years Nizami shut himself out still more from the outside world...

Door of my house against the world I close...

like lofty sky, with bolt, bar... both of those!

I do not know how the universe is revolving...

what goes on in it of that good or evil thing.

I'm like a dead body with the soul of a man...

but not journeying with those in the caravan.

Each breath... a hundred heart-aching blows:

every moment until I sleep I hear its echoes.

Not a one do I know who in soul and body...

who, as dear as himself is also holding... me.

His thoughts turn to his son still living away from him, his own mortality and immortality...

Many that like me are in the grave sleeping...

that all must sleep there none is remembering.

Ah my fresh young partridge, me please recall

when by head of my tomb your footsteps fall,

and look at the grass growing out of my clay,

my simple pallet broken down, fallen away...

dust of my couch blown away by the wind,

by one same age as me not brought to mind.

On that heap of ruins lay down your hand...

and in your mind my pure spirit understand;

shed over me a tear in your dwelling far away,

and on you I'll shed light from heaven's way;

to me you'll pray for whatever requires speed,

I'll be your surety that prayer will be fulfilled.

You send me a blessing, I'll send one to you;

come... and I'll come down from above to you.

Be thinking of me as one who like you is alive

and I'll come in spirit if to me you also arrive.

Don't think of me as one who lost his friend,

I'll look on you... if me you don't comprehend.

He informs us that he has forty times observed the forty days'
fast and seclusion and a thousand times given himself up to
solitude. Nizami reproaches himself for his own meekness...

How long will you remain as frozen as ice?

How long be dead like a drowned mouse?

Like prickly rose, abandon your softness...

show like the violet... colours diverseness.

There's a place in which a thorn is proper,

times when a little devilry one does prefer.

A Kurd once lost his small ass in Kaaba,

not seeing it in the courtyard, he shouted...

"Journey across desert was a very long one;

the mystery of losing it here tell this one!"

After these words behind him he looked...

and he saw the ass, and seeing it smiled,

exclaiming: "I lost my ass from my side...

found it because I shouted loud and wide."

But poetry remained from then on his chosen companion and the lofty consciousness of being one of its elect comforted him for being misunderstood and against verbal assaults. His time was divided between contemplation and reading. In the night, in which a happy vision first gave him a fresh impulse to a new production, this was his employment. His favourite occupation was in studying Firdousi's masterpiece *Shah-nama* or 'Book of Kings' and he had even formed the plan of filling the gaps in it and of working out the subjects not contained in a volume that as a supplement to the great heroic poem should in a similar manner bear the title of the 'Glory Book of Kings,' or briefly... the 'Glory Book'. As he recounts he had already worked on it for forty days. He speaks in the following terms of the work that he had in view and then abandoned...

> The ancient poet, the master of Tus... Firdousi,
>
> knew how to adorn his verse like a bride to see...
>
> in that book that he composed of pearls, threaded,
>
> he left many things unsaid... he might have said.
>
> But if all deeds done in olden times he'd written,
>
> to some it might have seemed too... overblown:
>
> so, he never wrote down what he did not prefer...
>
> saying what could not be omitted, nothing other.
>
> With regard to friends, he thought it a meanness
>
> to enjoy by himself those pleasantries... no less.
>
> And so, Nizami, who had strung many a gem...
>
> and wielded his reed in victories ad-infinitum,
>
> found in that treasury many a pearl unstrung...
>
> and them nicely in his own balance, he hung...
>
> giving them happy voice in his Book of Glory,
>
> restoring freshness to that... almost-lost story.

Nizami appears also to have promised himself much from this work. Soon deeper reflections made him give up this plan and while he remained thinking of the heroic-saga he wanted to create something new.

He decided that from him the world ought to receive no work resting on the production of another. His inspiration for this change comes from the mouth of Khizer* (see note at end of this chapter), who comes to him and among other things says the following...

I heard that in the 'Book of Kings' you desired

a spring... that from it, a fresh water welled.

Hear what the wise men of old used to say...

"Two holes in same jewel? One doesn't stay!"

Since you in your art can invent a new model,

without a reason don't on the worn-out dwell.

When you've the power to go choose a maiden,

do not descend to marry a widow... a burden!

While writing this Introduction to the first book of the two Alexander books... *Iqbal-nama*, 'Book of Fortune', of nearly 7000 couplets, Nizami took the advice offered in the last couplet and got married again... to another young, unnamed princess!

Khizer (or agent of Charge-man Perfect Master of the Age)...
(see note at end of chapter) then counsels him to take as the
subject of his new poem, the history of Alexander (of which of
course in the first book Khizer towards the end plays a very
significant role)...

Buy your jewels from the mine of Alexander,

even Alexander will of them be a purchaser:

when the world's monarch your work buys...

how quickly, your work will reach the skies!

To do this he decides the work must have a threefold division...
setting forth Alexander as conqueror of the world, Alexander as
philosopher and Alexander as a prophet...

From three seeds, scattered by hand of wisdom,

I will rear a tree of that is of a good proportion.

The first to that Monarch I will be dedicating...

to his deeds of so many kingdoms conquering:

and then I'll adorn my verses with Wisdom...

renewing freshness, the old chronicles from;

thirdly, I will knock at the door of prophecy...

for God called him to be a prophet, obviously.

Three entrances I've made, each to a rich vein,

on each I've no small worry, that's made plain.

But, it was obvious from the last couplet that he could not hold to this arrangement of three parts and so he bound the two last divisions, so closely related, into one. As the groundwork of the double division, he took the two journeys that he caused his hero to make through the world, the first as conqueror, the second as prophet. That he came to this resolution while he was still working on the first part is shown by this conclusion...

When the king returned to the Greeks' throne,

carrying in hand the key of happiness alone,

he gathered together great stores of learning,

opening the door of divine understanding...

but when he was called to office of a prophet,

he away from being in command he didn't let.

Again he prepared provisions for his journey,

tearing from mind desolation of the worldly.

Twice he paraded the earth as a conqueror...

through cities, mountains, plains and more:

and this time he saw, examining each piece:

cultivated, uncultivated, ended with Greece;

again he travelled its roads, pathless places,

showed light, like sun and moon, in all places.

Nizami's masterful atmospheric recreations of battlefields can be glimpsed in this account of the battle in 331 B.C. at Arbela between Darius and Alexander.

Roar of the lion came from bugle's loud blowing:

blaring of trumpets caused brains to be reeling.

With cracking sound whips were coming down,

the studded sky is pierced by that sharp sound.

Rushing noise of charging troops on battlefield,

reserves hustling... bustling to take the field!

Earth seemed to crackle... split in such a way:

"Is'rafil's blowing the horn of Judgment Day".

Fog, seeming impenetrable, sky was covering...

rein of safety in hand was no more remaining.

From dust... helmets, saddles difficult to see:

earth was sky, sky earth: all was topsy-turvy!

Earth was down and up on that terrible day...

blood ran to fish... dust to moon found a way.

On battlefield... from hoofs such dust flew up

that six climates... eight heavens were setup.

Shrieks of wounded a heart would be breaking,

from lassoes nooses soldiers were suffocating.

Unceasingly in, out that monster... the arrow,

had no rest to be lying in the string of the bow.

Nizami completed this first part of the Alexander book in the year 1200 and would immediately start work on the second part that he would complete on the 31st of May 1202... he was at that time about 62 years old and would live another seven years.

During the writing of the first book of Alexander... Nizami, as stated before, married for the third time. But within a few years she too would pass away and in writing the second book on Alexander he would lament his misfortune when it came to his love life...

My fate is strange, when the words come out:
when I make an old story... new, throughout!
When I pour out the sugar in that word-party,
another sweetly smiling bride... is lost to me.
When I concocted the sweet halva of Shirin...
the halva of my home was gone from therein.
When the treasure of Layla I had enclosed...
another bride to Paradise has given this lover.
My grief for each bride's so great that I doubt
I can write what Rome and Russia are about.
That I do not remember past sorrows is best...
so that this story I can enjoy inside my breast.

Nizami was justified in claiming for Alexander, as a main motive of his actions in this poem, his role as a prophet. The poet's religious nature could be satisfied only when the hero of his new work is not merely the ideal of a hero... has not merely reached the highest step of wisdom, but also possessed that state which in the eyes of the loyal Muslim is the highest on earth... that of prophecy. But in doing this he had also significantly enlarged the scope of his subject. That Nizami left nothing unexplored, that he drew together everything within his compass which bore upon his subject, is shown particularly by the following couplets...

When with much trouble I undertook this story,
words flowed freely but road wound intricately.
Traditions of that king who had ruled the world
I found no one scroll that had it fully chronicled.
Preserved legends were hoarded like a treasure...
scattered abroad... with difficulty I did recover.
From every manuscript some worth came to me,
I bound and embellished it with jewels of poetry.
I filled up my store from the more recent history:
the Jewish and Armenian and also old Pahlevi.
I took from every grain that which was excellent,
and from each pod in the innermost kernel went;

I joined riches of one tongue to those of another,

and the mass into a complete whole I did gather.

From this statement we can see that apart from his mastery of Arabic and Persian he also knew these three other languages as well as all the other sciences... a truly universal man. According to Nizami, in this second book about Alexander... *Khirad-nama* or 'Book of Wisdom', consisting of over 7000 couplets, Alexander sets out on a second expedition through the world. After making proper arrangements he proceeds from Macedonia to Alexandria, then on to Jerusalem, then by way of North-Africa to Andalusia. While in North-Africa he desires to reach the undiscovered source of the Nile. After a long march across desert, over mountain

and valley, he comes at last to a steeply ascending mountain, in colour resembling 'green glass,' from which flows down the river Nile. Of the people sent up to explore not one comes back. At last a man is dispatched, accompanied by his son, with orders that, on arrival at the summit he should write what he has seen and throw down the paper inside a wooden tube to his son who is to wait for him as closely as possible below. The son returned without his father, but with a message...

He gave Alexander the paper and the writing did say...

"From the awe-inspiring, terrible difficulty of the way,

from terror my soul in me into a faint had almost fell

for I seemed to be slowly climbing my way into a hell!

Path suddenly became contracted into a hair's breadth,

and I knew whoever trod it became sure of his death.

Because from this path that was as slender as a hair

there seemed to be no way of coming back from there.

When I arrived at this rocky mound that is the summit,

I was utterly distressed by the obvious narrowness of it.

All I saw as I looked back down tore my heart to pieces,

and from its sheer drop my judgment totally freezes.

But... I see that on the other side the outlook is perfect:

delight upon delight... and a garden in every aspect:

full of fruit and grass and rosebushes and clear water,

the whole region resounds with birds' melodious twitter;

the air is so soft... and the landscape... ah, it's charming:

here, you might say... God, every wish will be granting!

On this side there is nothing existing but life and beauty,

on that other there is nothing but ruination and enmity;

here it looks like Paradise and there it resembles Hell:

so who'd desert Paradise to go back to Hell? Me, tell!

Think of that desert, through which we made our way,

look where we came from and where you all now stay.

Who would have the heart to leave this delightful spot

and again set foot on that difficult path? I would not!

So... here I will remain O king... and I'll bid you goodbye:

and may you from now on be happy... as I'm sure will I!"

*NOTE: Who or what Khizer was and is has almost been totally misunderstood by authors and commentators of Sufism and Persian literature and religious history. The first *Qutub* or Perfect Master, Adam, established an 'Office of Khizer' that goes with the subsequent roles of the Head of the Spiritual Hierarchy filled by the *Qutub-e-Irshad* or Chargeman Perfect Master of the Five Perfect Masters always on Earth... of course with the coming of the *Rasool* or Messiah (Avatar) this 'Office' becomes His responsibility. When one who has no Master and is a true seeker of God cries from the depth of his or her heart for help the Head of the Hierarchy of the time utilizes this office and either through Universal Mind directs the person nearest to the seeker to go to him and direct him to the Master... or the Master takes form in the presence of the seeker as a youth or old man and advises him what to do next. So, as this 'Office' or 'Role' has been utilized by God in Human Form since Adam... the incorrect view came about that Khizer was one particular person or Master... seemingly immortal. Khizer is always available because God is always on Earth in human form and can always open the 'Office of Khizer' when needed. In fact anyone can be Khizer for anyone could be used by the Master as a means to bring about this function's purpose. See my 'Khidr in Sufi Poetry', New Humanity Books, 2012.

Chapter 7.

The Divan of Nizami.

During the last seven years of his life Nizami must have composed many other shorter poems that were added to his already massive *Divan* (a collection of poems other than long *masnavis* gathered together in one book alphabetically under the last letter of the rhyme-word). Nizami's *Divan* was first collated by him about the time of writing 'Layla and Majnun' and was added to over the many years that followed until eventually at the time of his death it consisted of *ghazals, qasidas, ruba'is, qit'as,* etc. He says in an outburst against a copier of his poetry...

If I show my art in a ghazal, tunefully,

that one soon puts out a horrible copy;

if I should compose an elegant qasida,

rows of weak couplets he copies to see.

His eulogistic poems were not many. Kasvini writing shortly after his time states... "Nizami composed a beautiful *Divan,* the poems of which are for the most part of a religious, admonitory or ethical character and which contains indications of the initiated and their symbols."

Nizami's *Divan* is said to have contained over 20,000 couplets (approximately 4,500 poems) of which nearly all have been lost (one of the world's great literary tragedies)... only about 2000 couplets survive today. Of these, very few have been translated into English and I give my versions of a small number below in the hope that some day someone will remedy this lack of appreciation.

Among the *ruba'is* from his *Divan* the following *ruba'is* are a few of the survivors...

"May my words with you have value," I said,
"Patience in love God give to me too," I said.
You: "Why do you pray?" Me: "Your union!"
You replied, "May God give it to you, I said."

Who is going to be helping me if I should sigh?
Not much life anymore for me if patiently I try.
Each moment and breath I'm remembering you:
God, make none for another have such a desire.

As from dusk to dawn for life to stay is hopeless,
only seed worth sowing is the seed of goodness;

and because the world will not stay for anyone,

being kind to one's friends is best; this, I stress.

That heart without a beloved is miserable one:

without friend or beloved is difficult for anyone.

This little time you'll not be able to find again,

if you've a heart don't be without a beloved one.

Wine is the best thing of all consumed by man,

find pure wine found in temple ruins if you can:

as this world's a ruined place with nowhere not

ruined... be ruined, drunk, in the ruins O man!

Ever since the wine of love I tasted in your grief,

all pain you can imagine I suffered in your grief.

Making a long story short... I died in your grief.

Tell what I've seen? Enough said, in your grief.

Nizami was also one of the greatest masters of the *ghazal* and one can see why his writing was, apart from his quintet of *masnavis*, a major influence on the other great masters of the *ghazal*... 'Attar, Rumi, Sadi, Hafiz and Jami. Here are a few examples...

Dark is the world and difficult the way, so for awhile your steed

rein in and tell yours gross self to discover... your soul's need.

The ravens of flesh's desire expel from the garden of humanity

and gain a share for the soul's Bird... by such an unusual deed.

Since you are in the Master's inner circle discard the world...

in a gulp, countless flagons of mystical wine... fill your need!

Don't be half asleep amongst those ones who are Light-hearted:

when Winebringer is active, quickly take large cup: do the deed!

You see His Hell and His Heaven? Pay no attention to either:

place foot on Hell's head, draw circle around Heaven is decreed!

When you are drunk with that One's presence, pull up the tent

of heavens, shake cosmos' pole, sky's ropes pull down! Indeed!

Without feet travel His Path, without eyes see His beauty...

without ears hear His tale, without mouth. His wine you need.

O Nizami, what secrets these are that your mind is revealing!

Your mystery, who knows? Hold your tongue in word and deed!

I went to Winehouse last night but a way in I couldn't see,

I called and called but no one inside seemed to listen to me.

Either no Wineseller was awake or because I was nobody,

in there nobody cared to open the door for me... obviously.

When a quarter, more or less, of the night had passed by,

an imbiber stuck his head out of the window, turned to me

and he said... "How does it go with you... and who do you

want so late at night, it's very late, it's late can't you see?"

I shouted, "Open door!" He... "Don't be stupid, go away!

This isn't the time when door is opened by one for anyone:

be thinking, this isn't a mosque where door is always open

where you can come and go, push to the front deliberately:

it is Masters Winehouse, where drunks, Winebringers go

a place of light, wine and songs and sweetmeats, you see?

All religious communities in the world are here: Muslims,

Hindus, Zoroastrians, Christians, Jews, one community.

Listen, if you've anything to say, then first you should go

and make yourself dust under their feet... it is that easy!"

O beloved, radiant of face, whose loved bride, will you be?

Whose dignity praise, whose honour and pride will you be?

At evening you're shaded by awning your master's spread:

whose queen with grace, hair and scented hide will you be?

You are much sweeter than honey, no sherbet is sweeter...

whose stream with love's waves on each side, will you be?

O bright lamp in dark night, God guard you from evil eye:

life's breath, whose love caress, who beside... will you be?

You are gone... how can Nizami live with his grief, alone?

Now he is down, whose healer of pain inside, will you be?

Why love the world, as you are here for just a day or two:

when death catches you off guard, confused... that's you!

Pretty face, why are you so proud of your silver and gold?

None will be of use, no matter how now you them value!

Don't you think of when men will lower you into a grave?

All your friends will leave there, staying will be only you!

Where's Adam, where's Eve, or Joseph... where's Moses?

Where's Job, Zakariah's son, and Noah of the flood, too?

Where's Abraham and where's Ishmael? They've all been

eaten by the earth! You think that you alone stays... you?

Where now is Jesus the son of Mary who raised the dead?

Where is Solomon's glory... where has his throne gone to?

O Nizami, if you do know that the day of death will come,

prepare for the Judgement: what's the point in talking, too?

You keep asking how I am, what do you think, my friend?

My liver is in agony... heart, blood does drink, my friend.

You just be leaving this telling of the story of love to me:

you just be Layla, for I'm Majnun on the brink my friend!

Every day that arrives I keep crying and crying for you...

each day my crying out sounds louder, I think, my friend.

I have heard this... that you are being kind to your lovers:

am I outside Your lovers' circle or on the brink my friend?

Didn't you say if I fell down your hand would help me up:

are you wanting me to fall and to forever sink, my friend?

I was reading some of the ghazals of Nizami for you, but,

his charm doesn't have an effect on you I think, my friend!

I've fallen in love with you, tell me what should I do?

Should I come with a good or bad reputation to you?

For as long as I live with heart and soul you I'll seek:

until, either I fall by the wayside, or me you come to!

In this love I have for you all the city was my enemy:

who'll have mercy on me if forgiveness you don't do?

If I happen to see you my hand will touch your hair...

you must know one so in love has an excuse, do you?

I am so lost without you, may no other be the same:

I've not a way to you... no patience without you too!

A rare qasida of Nizami's that has survived...

I'm height of knowledge: my perfection's great, my fame is spreading...

my genius is like the heavens... earth, time and fate I am overpowering.

My breath is like the earth, it is like chimes of a bell that resonates...

my pen is glory's banner, called on to create and earth be conquering.

My proud forehead has become as powerful as Kai-Kobad's crown...

ah no, in comparison to my high place his palace is a lesser thing.

In the skies my brilliant sun arose to shine throughout all creation...

while this body keeps breathing its power won't ever be lessening.

In the world of poets my name is immortal, my fame full of glory:

my genius is here... palace where kings reign this master's missing.

My heart is huge and generous, a great storehouse of pure nobility...

it has seal of Truth upon it and great is the Truth inside it staying.

If I look at the writings of Zabur and my pride becomes overwhelming...

I wish to cut out his thought-thieving tongue that hate is causing.

My generosity often results in pity, I'm often saying kind things...

what I give exudes fresh beauty, youth's sweetness is ever enduring.

To ears of the people my ghazals are reaching in waves of harmony,

these poppy-coloured ghazals like wine make hearts be drowsing.

Everything moving in the distant starry sky I am making move...

I am water in the gold cup of Fortune while the sky keeps turning.

Tambourine I'll not hit unless necessary, drums a wedding announce...

when I speak out music is obsolete , instruments silent are remaining.

And if what I create has errors in the words, they remain exquisite...

if there are dregs in my wine, you'll still drink deep, it is so pleasing.

This new style of mine begins a new age, all old values are passed:

any new word coined is worthless, if in value to mine one's comparing.

I conquered the world's heart with my poetry's mysterious beauty...

from this glory and success, love and admiration I am now harvesting.

When I write, the great calligrapher Ibn Muqla my pen he coverts...

when clearness of my words are seen, Ibn Khan his poise is losing.

When I open my mouth to express wisdom, all people are overjoyed...

buds of roses open, as my spring frees them from wintry sleeping.

If my word isn't heard in its glory, the scene isn't lit by happiness,

no minstrel you'll see whose singing will cause spring to be appearing.

Pride in my work is reasonable, my pen's poetry is beauty, sublime...

you'll discover the exquisite lines when my couplets you're reading.

Mother-of pearl I am, good I am: I'm clearer than gems of crystal...

but, it troubles me some do me harm and take things I'm needing.

When I breathe deeply and freely it is like a floating light mist...

it warms, helping me to like pearls, these fine couplets be threading.

It is true that I am a star that is shining obliterating fierce enemies...

greater than art or inspiration, poets and philosophers are disappearing.

The style of Nizami is like a charger with a light leather bridle...

my grief's a heavy, hard stirrup... but my steed is perfectly galloping.

Nizami dropped his physical form on the 12th of March 1209, but lives forever through his poetry.

Not that long after his death one of Persia's greatest poets, Sadi, said of his passing...

Nizami's gone, our exquisite pearl, that Heaven in its kindness
formed of the purest dew, for the gem of the world... no less!
Calmly it shone in its brightness, but by world not appreciated:
Heaven, reassuming its gift... again in its shell laid it to rest.

And Jami, the last great poet of Persia in his masterpiece 'Joseph and Zulaikha' mournfully cries...

Where is Nizami? Where his soul-alluring poetry?
Delicate refinements of his genius full of subtlety?
He has gone... taking his place behind the screen,
and all but him... remaining outside it have been.
Since he withdrew, we have received no portion...
except those mystical words he took, every one.
None knew them except he who God is near...
whose true heart with the divine is made clear.
But he has escaped from these narrow byways,
to journey to where that sacred temple stays...
and, afraid of the captives taken in the snare,
he stays under the skirts of that Throne there.
He washed his soul from the image of diversity
seeking to fill it again with Mystery of Unity.

SELECTED BIBLIOGRAPHY

(Books in English... general and specific consulted while working on this book.)

POEMS OF MAJNUN, Translation & Introduction, Paul Smith, New Humanity Books, Campbells Creek, 2012.

LAILI AND MAJNUN: A Poem. From the original Persian of Nazami by James Atkinson. A.J. Valpy Publishers 1886. (A reduced version in archaic verse.)

THE STORY OF LAYLA AND MAJNUN by NIZAMI Translated from the Persian and edited by Dr. R. Gelpke. English version in collaboration with E. Mattin and G. Hill. Bruno Cassirer Publishers Ltd 1966. (A greatly reduced version in prose.)

LAYLA AND MAJNUN BY NIZAMI. Prose Adaption by Colin Turner. Blake Publishers 1997. (So close to the prose version of Gelpke that one wonders why he bothered.)

A NARRATION OF LOVE: An Analysis of the Twelfth Century Persian Poet Nizami's Layli and Majnun by A.A. Seyed-Gohrab. Netherlands 2001. (This is a wonderful and masterly book about Nizami's most popular work. Highly recommended.)

LAYLI & MAJNUN: Love, Madness and Mystic Longing in Nizami's Epic Romance, by Ali Asghar Seyed-Gohrab, Brill, 2003.

MAJNUN: THE MADMAN IN MEDIEVAL ISLAMIC SOCIETY by M.W. Dols, edited by D.E. Immish. Clarendon Press, 1992.

LOVE, MADNESS AND POETRY: An Interpretation of Majnun Legend by A. Khairallah. Beirut. 1980.

MAJNUN LAYLA OF SHAUQI A play, Translated by A.J. Arberry, Luzac, London 1933.

LEYLA AND MEJNUN by FUZULI. Translated by Sofi Huri. Introduction and Notes by Alessio Bombaci. George Allen & Unwin Limited 1970. (Of special interest are chapters 3 'The Legend of Majnun' and 4, 'Layla and Mejnun by Nizami of Ganja'.)

THE FIRE OF LOVE: The Love Story of Layla & Majnun by Nizami, Trans. by Louis Rogers, Writers Club Press 2002.

UNVEILING THE GARDEN OF LOVE: Mystical Symbolism in Layla Majnun & Gita Govinda, Lalita Sinha, World Wisdom Books, 2008.

LAYLA & MAJNUN: LOVE POEM, A Verse Play by Ismail, Kitab Books 1997.

LAYLA-MAJNUN: A Musical Play in Three Acts by Dhan Gopal Mukerji, Paul Elder & Co. San Francisco 1916.

THE STORY OF MAJNUN: An Opera Tragedy in One Act by Bright Sheng & Andrew Porter, G. Shirmer Inc., 1992.

NIZAMI: SELECTED POEMS, Translation & Introduction by Paul Smith, New Humanity Books, Campbells Creek, 2012.

A LITERARY HISTORY OF PERSIA by Edward G. Browne. Volume 2. Cambridge University Press. 1906 (See pages 400-411)

PERSIAN POETRY FOR ENGLISH READERS by S. Robinson. Printed for Private Circulation 1883. (See p.p. 105-246.)

A GOLDEN TREASURY OF PERSIAN POETRY by Hadi Hasan. Indian Council for Cultural Relations 1966. Delhi, (See p.p. 126-137.)

HISTORY OF IRANIAN LITERATURE by Jan Rypka. D. Reidel Publishing Company 1968. (See p.p. 210-217 and elsewhere.)

THE POETRY OF NIZAMI GANJAVI: Knowledge, Love, and Rhetoric. Edited by Kamran Talattoff and Jerome W. Clinton. Palgrave, 2000. (The first four chapters are of most interest as regards 'Layla and Majnun' esp. Chapter 1... 'A Comparison of Nizami's *Layli and Majnun* and Shakespeare's *Romeo and Juliet* by Jerome W. Clinton.)

MIRROR OF THE INVISIBLE WORLD: Tales from the *Khamseh* of Nizami by Peter J. Chelkowski, Priscilla P. Soucek and Richard Ettinghausen. Museum of Modern Art. N. Y.1973

MINIATURES ILLUMINATIONS OF NISAMI'S 'HAMSAH'. Edited by E. Yusupov. Introduction by Fazila Suleimova. Fan Publishers. Tashkent 1985. (Suleimova uses the important work of Bertels and Krymsky & Aliyev).

MAKHZANOL ASRAR: The Treasury of Mysteries of Nezami of Ganjeh Translated for the first time from the Persian, with an Introductory Essay on The Life and Times of Nezami by Gholam Hosein Darab. Arthur Probstain Pub. 1945.

THE TREASURY OF THE MYSTERIES BY NIZAMI Translation, Introduction by Paul Smith. New Humanity Books, Campbells Creek, 2010.

THE HAFT PAIKAR (The Seven Beauties) by NIZAMI OF GANJA... Translated from the Persian with a Commentary by C. E. Wilson. Vol. 1 Literal Translation. Vol. 2 Commentary. Probsthain & Co. 1924.

THE HAFT PAYKAR: A Medieval Persian Romance by NIZAMI GANJAVI. Translated with an Introduction and Notes by Julie Scott Meisami. Oxford University Press 1995.

THE SIKANDAR NAMA,E BARA, OR BOOK OF ALEXANDER THE GREAT by Abu Muhammad bin Yusuf bin Mu,ayyid-Nizamu-'D-Din, Translated by Captain H. Wilberforce Clarke. 1881. (Literal translation of the first of the two Alexander books.)

NIZAMI: MAXIMS, Translation & Introduction by Paul Smith, New Humanity Books, Campbells Creek, 2012.

NIZAMI: SELECTED POEMS, Translation & Introduction by Paul Smith, New Humanity Books, 2012.

DIVAN OF HAFIZ. Translated by Paul Smith. New Humanity Books 1986. Revised edition 2012.

DIVAN OF SADI: His Mystical Love Poetry. Translated by Paul Smith. New Humanity Books 2012.

GOD SPEAKS: The Theme of Creation and Its Purpose by Meher Baba. Dodd, Mead and Company. 1955 and revised edition 1973. (See p.p. 44-59.)

THE CONFERENCE OF THE BIRDS BY FARID UD-DIN ATTAR. Translated with an Introduction by Afkham Darbandi and Dick Davis. Penguin Books. 1984.

A THOUSAND YEARS OF PERSIAN RUBAIYAT: An Anthology of Quatrains from the Tenth to the Twentieth Century Along with the Original Persian by Reza Saberi. Ibex Publishers, Maryland. 2000. (Pages 210-211).

THE DIVINE WINE: A Treasury of Sufi & Dervish Poetry. Volume One. Translations. Introduction, Notes etc. by Paul Smith. New Humanity Books, Campbells Creek. 2010.

ANTHOLOGY OF CLASSICAL ARABIC POETRY Translation & Introduction by Paul Smith, New Humanity Books, 2010. (Pages 116-123).

Layla & Majnun

O Winebringer, you know that I worship the wine:

so... now let that delicious cup of wine... be mine.

That wine that is pure and is as still as my tears...

that's the destroyer of all of the lover's dark fears;

by you I am inspired and with you I become bold...

in the fiercest of fights my post I will always hold:

inspired by you, I will pluck away at the string...

and in rapture, of love and of pleasure... I will sing.

You will become like a lion that is seeking the prey

as you roam the glades where the wild deer stray;

and like you like the lion I too would like to roam,

to be bringing all the joys that I am seeking home;

with that pure wine, life is dear, a sweet treasure,

for I am feeling the thrills of every subtle pleasure:

hey Winebringer, bring that ruby wine to me now;

for its fine lustre is sparkling upon your fair brow,

and now, as it is flashing with a tremulous light...

it makes your laughing eyes become more bright...

hey, Winebringer... bring that liquid gem and see

its great and wonderful power bubbling inside me.

I have no important ancestors of whom I can boast
all of the traces of my descent have now been lost.
From our father Adam what is it that I do inherit?
Nothing... nothing, but a sad and troubled spirit?
Because all human life from the most ancient time,
has forever been marked with the guilt of a crime:
and mankind... still the betrayer and the betrayed
is always lurking like the spider in the cold shade:
but the wine, O that wine still plays a magic part,
lifting to the highest of spirits that drooping heart.
And so listen, O Winebringer, don't wait, but give
that blissful balm... upon which I continue to live.
Come Winebringer, bring juice of the purple vine...
bring, quickly bring to me the musk-scented wine:
for a swallow of that pure wine the memory clears
and is awakening all thought of those other years
when that blushing fiery dawn lit up the old sky...
and so fill that large cup with wine, fill it up high!
That wine... which to the feverish one's cracked lip
that by anguish is dry... when given to one to sip
imparts to that one a rapturous smile, and throws
a glorious veil over all of those distracting woes...

the wine, that bright lamp, that all night and day
is lighting us upon our dark and world-weary way,
strewing our path with choicest fruits and flowers
and brightens with happiness our fleeting hours...
and is lifting upon high the mind... now in elation,
to Jamshid's glory... to Jamshid's highest station.
But of those who are royal, it is better to beware...
because it's not for you their regal smiles to share:
smiles can often be deceitful... the fire looks bright
and is seen to shed a lucid and a dazzling light...
although it may seem attractive, it is also known
that the safety of one is dwelling... in flight alone.
The radiance of the lighted candle the moth tries...
but in the flame's burning heart tormented it dies:
and no one ever laments such a one's foolish pride
that with those of royal birth strives to be allied.
Winebringer bring, bring that musk-scented wine!
That wine is the key to joy, and it must be mine...
that wine is that key that will open wide the door
to the treasure of rapture's rich and varied store...
that, which makes one's mounting spirits be glad,
one can then feel that majesty of old Kai-Kobad.

Wine, which over the mind casts a wonderful spell
of an exquisite kindness... that... is indescribable,
and so now... because I am in the drinking vein...
bring Winebringer, bring that luscious wine again!
From the Vintner bring to me another fresh supply
and please don't ever let this drinker's lips be dry.
Come Winebringer... you are not old and not lame
and from the minstrel you will receive no blame...
let him wash from his heart the dust of all sorrow
and please let him play on and on until tomorrow;
let the bubbling sound of wine-cup delight his ear,
like some song coming from a paradisical sphere...

Once there lived among the Bedouin in old Arabia
a lord, a Syed... Omri, ruling over the Banu Amir.
No other lands flourished like his and the breeze
took the scent of his glory to its furthest reaches.
His success and his prosperity made him a leader
of many Arabs and he was as wealthy as Korah.
He helped the poor... his purse was always open:
to all strangers he was a generous host and when
he began a new venture he succeeded... as if good

luck he had like stone in fruit: this, he understood!

Although respected like a king... inside he seemed

like a candle, slowly consuming itself until, dead?

The great man's heart was eaten by a secret grief:

he had all he wanted... but no son had that chief.

What did glory, power, wealth matter... if one day

they'd all go, without an heir to make them stay?

Did the corn have to drop, the branch have to die?

If cypress fell... where would pheasant at night lie?

Where will lie happiness? Where is shade to nest?

He stays alive, who in his son is seen and blessed.

In this way this nobleman worried and the older he

became the greater became his need for a progeny.

For many years his alms and prayers were in vain

moon never rose, that seed's offshoot never came.

Still, he was never content to bow to his destiny

one wish not given... but all else he could not see!

That is how most of us are: if a prayer remains not

fulfilled... do we think it is what should be our lot?

We think we know, yet the future's veiled from us:

our fate's thread ends beyond the visible and thus

what today we mistook for a lock, keeping us out

may later be the key... that, which we had sought.
He desired the jewel he didn't have... so he prayed
and he begged until finally God his wish fulfilled.
He was given a boy who looked like a rose's smile:
the rose, whose petals keep opening all the while
one sleeps... like a diamond which can transform
the darkness of the world into a light... newborn!
Overcome, the happy father opened wide the door
of his great treasury. All would share in his store
of happiness... and this event was then celebrated
with shouts and blessings to parents were related.
The child was given to a caring nurse, so under her
careful eye he'd grow strong... and even stronger.
Each milk-drop in his body... a sign of faithfulness,
and each bite became in his heart a... tenderness.
Lines drawn on face to protect... magic on his soul:
this remained secret... hiding it, she knew her role!
The child looked like the moon after fourteen days
and so his parents gave him the name of... Qays.
A year passed... and his beauty grew to perfection:
as light cuts water, in his form... love's reflection.

So playful and joyful, year after year he flourished,
a flower... in childhood's happy garden nourished.
And when he turned seven the violet-coloured hair
of a first beard began to show on his cheek: there!
And when he had finally passed his first ten years
some spoke of his beauty like a fairy tale, in tears!
And whoever did happen to see him... even if only
from afar, called upon God to bless him, eternally.
Look now on where instruction pours on the mind
the light of knowledge... both simple and refined;
each leader of a tribe has his children there... each
is studying what the old, bearded sage can teach.
So it was here young Qays, his knowledge drew...
and he scattered pearls from his lips of ruby hue...
it was here, of a different tribe and a gentler way,
a lovely maid of tender years came one fatal day:
her intelligence in its early bloom was to be found
and her quiet body was clothed simply, but sound.
Bright as morning was her cypress shape and eyes
deer-dark, were seen by all with fondest surprise:
when this Arab moon her bright cheek revealed...
a thousand hearts were won... no pride or shield,

could stop her beauty: it was impossible to resist!

She was given to enthrall, to charm: one, the most!

Her long, flowing curling locks were black as night

and she was called... Layla, that heart's delight...

just one glance and the nerves became distraught,

just one glance, bewildered became each thought:

and, when over young Qays, love's blushing rose

spread its rare sweetness, from him fled all repose:

a tumultuous passion danced upon his hot brow...

he wanted only to win her, but he knew not how:

he gazed upon her perfect cheek and as he gazed,

love's flaming candle intensely inside him blazed.

And soon the same pleasure fed each other's heart:

love had won them and they never dreamt to part.

And while the other students looked at their books

these two stared back and read each other's looks:

while the other schoolmates for distinction strove

and thought of fame... they, only thought of love:

while the others various places in books explored,

those two sat and stared... the adorer and adored!

And science for them now had no charms to boast,

and learning for them had all of its meaning lost...
their only taste was for love and love's sweet ties,
and writing *ghazals*... poems to each other's eyes.
Yes... love triumphant had come, engrossing both
the hearts and thoughts of the girl and the youth,
and while being overcome by that delicious thrill,
smiles and joyful tears both faces and eyes did fill.
Then in quiet secret talking they passed the hours:
their love was like the season, like the fair flowers
freshly strewn upon the path now opening to their
sweet, melting words that are soft as Summer air.
Immersed in love... young, and yet it was so deep,
they hoped all suspicion would be lulled to sleep...
and that no one would see their loving condition...
that gossips would not put them under suspicion,
and thinking like this, they then anxiously prayed
that their love would not to any others be relayed,
wishing the others saw what they no longer were,
though all could see their hearts as one they were.
But by a worldly prudence that was uncontrolled,
in their every glance... their true feelings they told:
because true love never thinks of knowing the skill

of veiling those passionate looks of lovers, at will.
And when those black ringlets of a thousand curls,
and those lips of ruby... with those teeth of pearls,
and those dark eyes flashing, so quick and bright,
like the lightning on the brow of the darkest night
when such charms as these their power display...
and they then steal one's bewildered heart away...
can any man living, openly lying, so coldly seem
to be totally unmoved as if by only a mere dream?
Young Qays saw her great beauty, saw her grace,
and he saw the soft expression on her perfect face
and as he gazed, he gazed and gazed again, again
he gazed: so, distracted became his burning brain:
then, no moment's rest he had by day or by night
because Layla was permanently there, in his sight.
But, when the fateful separation eventually came,
more brightly glowed this ardent lover's flame...
and Layla, in her deepest sorrow was also caught,
weeping about what upon them, Fate had brought.
He, now wandered wildly through lane and street,
walking like one insane as if he was about to meet
something which all of his searching couldn't find,

what could happen never crossing his upset mind.
His chest, it heaved with his groans and his sighs,
and tears were seen to be gushing from his eyes...
and still he was struggling, still trying to conceal
that terrible anguish that he was doomed to feel:
and now... so mad with all of this excessive grief,
into the lonely desert he wandered for some relief.
Eventually... as the morning dawned he ran away,
upon his head and his feet no covering did he lay...
and during each night, with a great growing pain,
the whip of absence lashed him again, and again.
And then along the secret path he frantically goes
to where that mansion of Layla's parents arose...
then he kissed the mansion's door and in that kiss
he imagined he'd quaffed the cup of a divine bliss.
How fast his feet moved to his sweetheart's place,
it was as if a thousand wings quickened his pace...
but after he had his loving devotions to her paid...
many thousands of thorns... his way back delayed.
This young lover who from his beloved was parted
now wandered, so depressed and broken-hearted:
he sank, like the sun without any ray, way down...

like Khosrau... but without a throne, or a crown.
With his long tangled hair and a chest now bare,
his slim body unshielded from the scorching air...
this unfortunate youth, so absorbed in love's grief,
hoped that with his friends he'd find some relief...
a few of them, by a strong affection to him bound,
in midst of his troubles still faithful he now found.
Eventually... a useless refuge, friendship's smile...
his lovesick heart was beguiled for a short while...
and once again he rushed out into the wilderness,
for all he loved in life had vanished and in distress
he called out her magical name... but she was not
to be seen anywhere, and none of her family... not
anyone could he see in that wild, that lonely land:
he called her many times and then did understand
that no one had heard him crying... for her in vain:
not one dear reply, that poor wretch could obtain.
For Layla had, with all her family been taken away
to far off Najd mountains... where they'd all stay.
Where she could think of only that one she loved...
and so her love grew deeper, as she slowly moved

restlessly around that wild mountainous retreat.
Her poor lover Qays went looking for her: to meet
her he looked in the rosy bower, each silent glade
where the tall palm-trees gave a refreshing shade.
He desperately called aloud her name once again...
again he called his beloved, again... again in vain:
his voice was not heard anywhere, on every side...
it was always his echo that to him sadly replied...
Layla, Layla, Layla! Her name rang out all around
as if all there were fascinated by its magic sound.
Now, dejected and forlorn, the quickly-falling dew
glistening on his bony cheeks, a pale yellow hue...
lonely, through the grove and meadow he strayed,
and with his grief to speak the rocks were made...
'My beautiful Layla... has she now gone for ever?'
Could he keep thinking that? O no... never, never!
While an agonizing pain was stabbing in his chest
he to the morning-breeze these words addressed...
"O breeze of the morning, so fresh and so sweet...
will you go to my beautiful beloved to kindly greet
and, then nestling in her glossy, long flowing hair,
my tender-most thoughts, my love for her declare?

Will you... while you are in her black curls playing,
their intoxicating scent... their perfume smelling,
tell to that loved one, my fair soul-seducing maid,
how from grief of separation down low I am laid!
And please... so gently whisper in her precious ear
this message that I give you, to her make it clear:
'Your lovely form is staying always in my sight...
in thoughts through the day and dreams by night,
for this poor one, who is in spirits sad and broken,
your cheek's dark mole would be the happy token:
that black mole... that always adds to each glance
a magical spell for which I can't take the chance...
for, that one who sees all of your melting charms
and does not feel his soul clasped inside his arms
bursting with such passion, with such rapture, all
that speaks of love's deepest and wildest thrall...
would have to be as Káf's summit, like ice... cold,
and probably not born out from the human mould.
Let the one who is not moved by charms like yours
give up his life, for no real life through him pours!
Those lips of yours are sugar, so heavenly sweet...
let only these lips... your sweet pouting lips meet!

The balsam for this heart's pure delight they shed
and their radiant colour is like the ruby: ruby-red.
The evil-eye has now struck out at my poor heart,
but it was your beauty that hurried the fatal dart:
and there have been many flowers, of richest hue,
that did fall and then perished where they grew...
but your great beauty is like the sun in brightness,
your form's an angel of Paradise in pure lightness:
you are an incalculable treasure... which poets say
even all of the heavens would gladly steal away...
'Too good, and too pure, upon this earth to stay!' "

As the morning broke, the sun with a golden light
eclipsed those twinkling stars, all silvery white...
and Majnun, quickly rising... now eagerly pursued
a pathway that wound towards Layla's solitude,
his heart full of longing... and, as he went along,
his lips breathed softly some passionate song...
some favorite poem... which tenderly expressed
the feeling that was always in his anxious breast.
In his imagination her image he continued to see,
no shadowy cloud was veiling her clear beauty...

He saw her as fresh as the morning's scented air:
he... himself, was exhausted by his constant care:
he saw her blooming just like the blushing rose...
he himself... was dejected by his numerous woes;
he saw her like a kind of angel, so light and pure...
himself, he kept burning away like an iron on fire;
her long black curls flowing loosely to the ground:
his tangled and matted hair by his love was bound.
Sick with sorrow of separation he passed his days,
pouring his soul out in songs, about her... always.

Now his friends, to whom his grief is well known,
about this great change in him all begin to moan:
they, alarmed to hear the hurting voice of him still
in this mood full of madness, that does forever fill
the night's cold breeze with his cries of his woes:
the more sorrow he expresses... the more it grows.
They all tried to soothe his poor bewildered mind,
where reason once was seen to be there enshrined;
and his father, who had for his son a father's love,
his dear son's sad sorrows he tried hard to remove
by giving him maxims: good advice, full and clear,

and... understanding counsel, for his son to hear.
But, although good counsel and the best of advice
may often be the cause of one going to Paradise...
once that love has a heart engrossed... enthralled,
all counsel and all advice is... completely wasted,
and... for that weeping Majnun not a single word
of his poor father's intelligent counsel he heard...
Ah! Tell me, when did prudence ever have control
over the intoxicated madness of a love-lost soul?
Disconsolate, his poor father to his harem rushes:
"How to stop the tears that from my son gushes?
And tell, what has taken away the sparkling moon
of commonsense from my poor son so very soon?"
The answer of the women... all the old and young,
was finally ready, given... quivering on the tongue:
"His fate's fixed because his young eyes have seen
the many charms of his enraptured heart's queen,
in all their winning power that's possible to unfurl
and his heart's now a captive to that Arabian girl.
And so... what kind of relief can you now supply:
what to that bleeding lover who is doomed to die?
You can do nothing other than to fulfil his desires

and to do this, a father's generous aid he requires.
It is best that those two unite in the bands of love;
only *that* his mad intoxication will truly remove!"
These words, (because women's words can convey
a spell... that can change the night into the day),
upon Majnun's father's troubled life were a balm
he hoped would his son's love-fever make calm...
these words did relieve Majnun's father's heart,
and instant comfort to his thoughts did impart.
Resolved at once he was, and he now with speed
marshaled his followers... every man with steed;
and... finally with all following he wends his way
to the home of lovely Layla... without any delay.
Quickly riding up to them the guard asks him this:
"You come here now as friends or foes... which is
the reason why you are here, whatever can it be?
The real reason please immediately convey to me;
because not one, unless he is a sanctioned friend,
are allowed to pass this boundary that I defend."
This challenge, it then touched Syed Omri's pride,
and he swallowed and in a calm manner replied...
"I come here in peace and friendship, and propose

all future chances of a feud between us, to close."

To Layla's father, who had approached, he said...

"The nuptial feast for them should now be spread

because my son with his thirsting heart has seen

your pure fountain, with margin around it green,

and every fountain that's clearly pure and bright,

gives to the heart that is thirsting a pure delight.

That fountain my son now demands. With shame,

possessing great power and wealth and also fame,

I... his father, to his ridiculous temperament bend

and, now... I do humbly ask for his fate to blend

with one who is so obviously inferior. Need I tell

of my own high lineage... that is known so well?

And if towards sympathy my heart should incline,

or... towards vengeance, still the means are mine.

My vast treasure, countless arms, can amply bear

me through the terrible toils of a long desert-war;

but in this case you're the merchant, peddler-chief,

and I, I am the purchaser: so come, sell... be brief!

Now listen... if you are wise, accept this advice...

sell immediately... you'll receive a princely price!"

The father of Layla took note of his haughty tone,

but he smoothly answered, "It is not on us alone
that this nuptial union depends, but on Heaven,
by which all power and right and truth are given.
However right our reasoning may seem to appear,
we are still beset by endless mistakes down here;
and an offered friendship may by chance become
the harbinger of terrible strife... and of the tomb;
madness is neither a sin nor a crime, as we know,
but who would be linked to madness... or to a foe?
Your son is mad... and so, his senses first restore:
in constant prayer the aid of the heavens implore.
But while an ominous gloom's pervading his brain,
disturb me not with this ridiculous request again.
The jewel of sensibility not one purchaser can buy,
and treachery in place of sense one cannot supply.
You have my reasons, know all this talk is over...
keep them in mind and now trouble me no more!"
Astonished and confused... his heartstrings torn,
to be met like this, scoffed at, the object of scorn,
Syed Omri... towards his many followers turned,
his dark brow with kindled anger fiercely burned,
but deciding there was nothing more to do or say,

indignant as he was... to home he made his way.
And now the question is... for a disordered mind
what medicine can this one who loves him find?
What magic power exists... or, what human skill
is there to cure heart and mind that's never still?
The art of necromancer was one way they tried...
they used charms and potions to win that bride,
and make her father's hard heart finally relent...
as if by Heaven in pity a consent could be sent...
but they were useless efforts. They now address
to Majnun kind words, mind to soothe and bless,
and now quietly urge into his young unwilling ear
(which is really treason and death for him to hear)
"Another love... another love of ours, a nobler race,
unmatched in beautiful form, unmatched in grace;
alluring, sweet-talking and the ways of an angel;
her every glance attracts the heart with a spell...
an idol to glorify of such high transcendent worth,
with charms that would eclipse one of royal birth,
whose balmy smoldering lips like the rubies glow;
sugar, milky sweet, her words like soft music flow:
she is adorned in all the pride of flowering Spring,

and her robes around her richly scented air fling...
yes, sparkling with gold and with gems she seems
to be the bright perfection of dear lover's dreams.
And now, why, with such a superior prize at home,
for charms inferior would you to a stranger roam?
Make all thoughts against doing your duty depart,
and wisely banish the Layla girl from your heart."
When Majnun saw all of his bright hopes decay...
their fairest blossoms fading... away, away, away;
and friends and father, who might once have been
kind and possible go-betweens, then rush between
him and the only hope he had that had so far shed
one ray of comfort...   around his distraught head
he beat his hands on walls, his garments he tore,
and threw the ropes that bound him onto the floor
in many pieces and then distressed and very angry
seeking out a path to the dark wilderness went he,
and there he wept openly and he sobbed out loud,
no longer seen by a gazing, a disapproving crowd.
His eyes were flowing tears and soul was aflame,
repeating over and over again his Layla's name...
and Layla! Layla! Layla... echoed from all around:

everything was dwelling on that rapturous sound.
In the rags of a wanderer he recklessly did stray...
nothing on feet or head he wandered on his way;
and... as memory of her touched his feverish brain,
he murmured some love-bewildered, poetic strain:
always her name was there... lying on his tongue,
and 'Layla' still throughout grove and forest rung.

This sad inmate of the wild desert soon discovered
his whole body and face was with dust covered...
exhausted by his mountain of grief, by separation
he sat wearily down, taking note of his situation:
"Estranged from my friends," he, weeping cried...
"Way home is dark; but, if Layla were at my side,
how blessed would her poor lover be... yet family
of mine are ashamed, friends no longer know me.
O no! I held that cup of wine in my hand but when
it fell out of my hand, it smashed into pieces then:
and so it all goes like that... just like the winecup
the hope of a life in a dark moment, all broken up!
You who have never experienced such devastation,

who've never had to leave place of heart's elation,
who have peaceful mind with no worries lurking...
what could you know of a heart, that is breaking!"

But Majnun, he no longer had the strength to flee:
falling upon his knees in the dust... he desperately
began calling to his Layla... who was so far away,
and implored her to help him... "I've fallen... say
what I should do? O my beloved... come and take
my hand. I can't endure this, oh... for God's sake
I'm of more use to you alive than dead... so now be
generous, send a greeting... message to revive me.
You're imprisoned I know, but why imprison you?
I'm the madman, I should be held. Bind me to you:
wind again your curls round my neck: they're torn,
yet, I remain your slave... now help *us*, to be born!
This is a cruel game, so end it... go lift your foot so
that I may kiss it... nothing remains as it seems so.
It is not right to sit in the corner with arms folded,
doing nothing... take pity on me, for a man rested
has no pity for a one exhausted... but a man, able
to fulfil all hunger... inviting a beggar to his table

knows nothing about starvation and yet... he may
eat a few morsels to honour his guest! Now I say,
that both human beings, you, as well as... even I:
if you're a blossoming tree, a dry thorn-bush am I!
O peace of my soul... where are you? Why do you
take my life, other than my love, what sin do you
see my heart: this heart asks for your forgiveness.
Of a thousand nights give me but one: happiness!
Look, everything else I've gambled away and lost:
do not say 'No'... if you are angry with me, toss
that fire of your anger into the water of my tears.
I'm a star, my new moon... driven to strange fears
by this longing to see you and my only companion
is my poor shadow, with him I dare no communion
for I am afraid he might sometime become a rival.
If only your shadow stayed with me, but... ah well
you've taken it away... and my heart and my soul
have gone... and what did I get in return? O soul,
what is left for me, hope? A thirsting child may in
some dream see hands offering a gold cup, but, in-
between when sleeping, waking... what remains?
All he can do... is suck fingers to quench his pains.

Nothing can kill my love for you: a riddle without
any solution, a code which no one can ever shout!
It entered with my mother's milk and it will leave
with my soul... no matter what you may believe!"
Worn out after this, he fell down upon the ground,
and there in tears that mournful youth was found
by those who'd traced his wanderings: gently they
now to Syed Omri's home that form did convey...
his father and fellow tribesmen around him moan,
and all of them weeping, make his grief their own;
then telling stories... bring back to memory's eye
the wonderful tale of Majnun's life from infancy to
the flattering promise of those boyhood days...
and find the wreck of hope, on which they gaze...
they then and there decide... that Mecca's sacred
shrine will help his reason be completely restored;
that blessed boon that to mortals had been given,
that arc of the earth and also that arc of heaven...
that holy Kaaba where the Holy Prophet prayed,
where waters of Zam-Zam yield their saving aid.

And now has arrived the season of the pilgrimage,
and now assemble merchants, chieftain and sage,
with vows and offerings... for on that spot divine
many a thousand will circle that splendid shrine.
And now, meant only for that high purpose, await
Syed Omri's many camels, all ready at his gate...
now around each neck the tinkling bells are hung,
and rich tasseled housings on each back are flung.
Now Majnun, faint and caring not what may be,
is on a litter placed... a sad and sorry sight to see!
He is tenderly caressed while swiftly borne along
by the rough moving camel, so fleet and so strong.
The desert is soon passed and now Mecca's bright
and glittering minarets rise up to meet their sight;
where golden gift and sacrifice and many a prayer
secure absolution that is eagerly sought for there.
His father, upon entering that all-powerful shrine,
prays... "Have mercy, O Allah, on me and mine!
Oh... and from my son this frenzied mood remove,
save him... save him from the destruction of love!"
Majnun on hearing this, that poor wayward child,
looked deeply into his father's face and he smiled,

honestly saying his life should conclusively prove
the ultimate truth and the holiness that is... Love.
"My heart is completely bound by beauty's spell,
and my love is permanent... it is... indestructible.
Am I to be made separate from my being, my soul:
from her for whom I alone breathe, my only goal?
What kind of friend could be wishing me to resign
a love that is so pure and that is so true as mine?
And even if I should like a candle happen to burn,
and almost into pale and shapeless shadow turn,
I'll never have any envy for the heart that is free:
forever be... Love's soul-encircling chains for me!"
The love that springs from the Beyond is blessed,
unholy passions stain the rest... it has been said;
that is not love that of some wild fantasy is born,
is never constant and always wants another form.
But the love that Majnun had wasn't of the earth,
it shone out forever and ever with the higher truth;
it was Layla's earthly form that raised the flame...
but, it was from the Beyond that inspiration came.

In heavy silence and deep sorrow his aging father
found that all his hope could be taken no further;
and so now back to his expecting tribe he turned
his slow steps again for Mecca had no power to
quench love's fire that in his son grew and grew.
No consolation was forthcoming, there's no relief
for this old man's heart-consuming, growing grief.
Months later sweet Layla's kinsmen now describe
to her father... that proud chieftain of their tribe,
a wild youth in the desert that's sometimes seen,
wearing only rags and acting madly he has been
seen stretching out his arms, his head is all bare,
and flowing loosely his mattered, his filthy hair:
"In a manner, that reeks of madness," they say...
"he wanders aimlessly here and there, each day...
it is noticed that often, with one fantastic bound
he then dances, or prostrate he hugs the ground...
or, in a voice that would cause any a soul to move
he cries out the melting songs of his denied love:
songs which, when sung in tones that are so true,
thousand hearts the sound would at once subdue.

He speaks, and all who are nearby listen and hear
words which ever in their memory they hold dear;
it is us and it is you who must endure the shame...
and dear Layla's blushes when hearing his name."
Now their chieftain on hearing this is full of wrath
and angrily threatens to cross the mad one's path.
Fortunately, preventing anything brutal he may do
to Seyd Omri's groves of palms, the news it flew;
immediately, his father sent off a few chosen men
to seek that one long-lost son. They, finally then
crossed open plains, waded through thickets deep
and rode down deep valleys, up mountains steep,
exploring here and there with many searching eye
where man might be able to pass or be able to lie,
overcome by grief or by death. But it was in vain
that their sight towards each side they did strain:
no Majnun's voice, no form did they see to cheer
anxious hearts: far, near, beasts growls they hear.
Sadly, they decide Majnun must be lost or dead...
and, bitter tears of anguish by every man is shed.
But he, that wanderer straying far from his home,
did not discover from those beasts a living tomb;

his passion that was so pure and its sacred flame
their animal fierceness seemed to be able to tame;
both the tiger and a ravenous wolf passed by him,
and the cruel hyena would never come near to him.
It seemed to be, that as if ferocious spirits to quell,
his thin and tortured form had become invisible...
or, it could be, that it carried a life-protecting spell.

Suddenly, upon a gurgling, emerald fountain brink
Majnun stooped, its clear rippling waters to drink;
at that same moment his despairing friends spied
him lying along that murmuring fountain's side...
still wailing out his sorrows and in his feeble voice
he dwelt, ever dwelt, upon his heart's sole choice.
They noticed a wild emotion trembling in his eye,
his chest heaving with many a deeply-drawn sigh
and groans and tears and songs that in mind stay
all these he did... throughout his melancholic day.
And now he is stretched out on the burning sand,
a stone he has for pillow... now, raising his hand
he breathes prayers for Layla and now once again
the desert echoes with some his mournful refrain.

As wine deprives us of senses of which we boast,
so reason in love's maddening intoxication, is lost.

At last, brought to home again, he dreads to meet
his father's frowns and he bends to kiss his feet...
then gazing wildly he rises up and then he speaks
and in piteous tone his father's forgiveness seeks:
"Sad my fate, now overcast is my youthful dawn,
my rose's leaves and my life's sweet buds are torn.
I sit in complete darkness with ashes on my head,
to all of the world's alluring pleasures I am dead;
what poor excuse can I give to soothe your mind?
Listen, you are still my father, O please be kind!"
Syed Omri, his unchanging love he tried to prove
by the folding into his chest this child of his love,
he exclaimed... "My boy! It grieves me so to see
that reason is still lost to you... in the dark misery
a fire is burning away every single hanging thread
from which each nerve inside you... you are made.
Sit down... and from your eyesight completely tear
out the poisonous thorn that rankles inside there...
it is best that we should to happiness now incline,

but please don't let it happen because of the wine:

it is right that desire should be filling your breast:

but not such great desire that will stop one's rest.

Please, remain no longer under this grief's control,

no longer listen to an enemy that taunts the soul:

from now allow wisdom each movement to guide,

for mistakes do greatly swell this affliction's tide

Although it is love that has set your heart on fire,

and still your heart burns with unquenched desire,

do not let yourself be despairing of some remedy,

because from a mere seedling springs a shady tree:

from hope going on and on there follows gladness

which that deep despair had once lost in sadness:

and so my son... associate with the wealthy, they

will show you to glittering wealth... and the way

that a wanderer like you *were* never gathers store,

and advice for you now is: be a wanderer *no more*.

Wealth will open every door and wealth also gives

orders... and much homage wealth also receives:

so my advice is: be patient then, and patience will

by slow but sure degrees all your large coffers fill.

That river that keeps on rolling... deep and broad,

one time it was only a narrow stream that flowed;
the high mountain that now comes easily in view,
its enormous height from a small foundation grew.
The one who is impatient, that one who hurries on
hoping for fabulous gems... he obtains only stone:
it is shrewdness and cunning that gains the prize,
while the essence of wisdom only in poverty lies.
Look at that fox with that crafty, that subtle mind
how he leaves that wolf's dullness so far behind...
you should be discreet and your thoughts employ,
and the inviting pomp the world offers you, enjoy.
When one is searching for wealth from day to day
that useless passion of love will quickly die away:
one living in his senses makes diseases his guest,
that one nourishes many a scorpion in his breast.
Since when has your heart O so worthless grown,
that it has become the cruel sport of... only one?
Keep it from a woman's scathing tongue, and still
obedient let your heart stay to your own free will;
and listen, always take seriously a parent's voice,
make *him*, not those who're your enemies rejoice."
Majnun slowly replied: "Father! My father, still!

All power has left me and I can't change my will:
all the moral counsel that you have given to me...
(To this one who can never from his bondage flee)
is useless to me... because it is *no* choice of mine,
but it is Fate's decree, that I to my fate do resign:
do I stand alone? Look around you, on every side
are broken hearts, that are by hardest luck tried:
shadows are not self-made: look, the silver moon
isn't self-stationed... but by the Almighty's boon.
Father, from the huge elephant's stupendous form,
to that of the poor ant and the smallest of worm,
through every grade of life all power that's given,
all joy or anguish comes from the Lord of Heaven.
I did not go out looking for misfortune but it came:
I did not look for the fire, yet my heart is all flame:
they ask me why I do not laugh and I don't smile,
though laughter is no sign of sanity all the while.
If I laugh... be in a merry mood with mouth agape,
while I'm laughing some secret may easily escape.
Once a partridge seized an ant and resolved to kill
that feeble creature with his sharp and horny bill...
when, laughing loud, the ant did exclaim... 'Alas!

Partridge, you? Are *you* such an unintelligent ass?
I am a mere gnat... and do you think you can float
a gnat's slight, filmy, texture down *your* throat?'
The partridge laughed at this tiny, unusual sound
and, laughing, dropped that ant upon the ground.
And so, he who would idly laugh will always find
some sorrow happen... it is so with all mankind.
The stupid partridge, laughing, lowered his crest,
and by that folly lost everything he'd possessed:
this poor old worker, which bears its heavy load,
must all his life long endure the same rough road;
no joy for him... in mortal aid there lies no trust,
no rest for him until death consigns him, to dust."

Here Majnun paused and then he wept; and now
those in the household stroke his furrowed brow,
and with all of their worried, unceasing eagerness
they try to take from him his soul's deep distress.
But grief, ever-corroding grief won't allow a quiet
thought and his wounded heart will him never let
have peace... and his family with each change in
his features try tracing what is happening within,

and their tears that don't help, their cheeks cover.
And a new anguish marks his face... much deeper,
his faded form now seems so haggard to the eye;
useless is task of his sorrows trying to remove...
for who can free the heart from... unchanging love?

A few days had passed and frantic he had grown,
and finally he burst out of this domestic prison...
and into the wild, vast, burning desert, still alone,
pouring out as from the morning bird newly risen,
came his latest ardent song of love. And not long
afterwards the mountains echoed with his song...
soon, drawn by the song's sounds sweet and clear,
crowds of listeners appeared and all hovered near:
they saw him standing tall as cypress does stand,
sharp piece of rock still tight in his bleeding hand;
a deep, wide, purple sash his waist bound around,
his bruised legs are still with a link of iron bound,
and yet even though, unencumbered was his gait:
all they all could only see, was his maniacal state.

Later, wandering he arrives at this spot of ground,
with groves of palms that is by poplars crowned...
a lively, lovely scene it is to please anyone's eye,
where flowers are blooming of every hue and cry.
Suddenly, turning around, he saw an axe applied
to a tall, beautiful cypress-tree and then he cried:
"Stop, gardener! Did love your heart ever control?
Was there a woman who had power over your soul
and when joy has thrilled in every glowing nerve,
have you not had a wish that feeling to preserve?
Does not a woman's love delight and... entrance,
and each blessing that fortune may give enhance?
Listen! Stop that lifted hand, that stroke suspend,
spare, spare that cypress-tree... and be my friend.
And why? Look there... and you be warned by me,
it is the form of Layla, graceful... full of majesty;
would you root up a likeness that is so complete,
and lay its poor branches, withering, at your feet?
What! Layla's form? No! Spare that cypress-tree;
let it remain, let it stay, living beautiful and free...
yes, let my prayers your feeling of kindness move,

and save that graceful shape of her, whom I love!"
The gardener dropped his axe, overcome by shame,
and left the tree to bloom, and tell of Layla's fame.

Layla in her beauty and her softness and her grace
far surpassed even the most loveliest of her race...
she was a fresh and a sweet softly-scented flower,
plucked by Angel of Paradise from her fair bower:
with heart-delighting rosebuds slowly blooming...
and a welcome light breeze of Spring's perfuming.
The magic that openly takes anyone's life that lies
in those deadly, blacker than black, delicious eyes,
when she gathers them into one amorous glance...
it pierces the heart just like the sword or the lance;
the prey that should happen to fall into her snare,
for the rest of life must mourn and struggle there.
Her eyelash speaks with a thousand kinds of bliss,
and her ruby lips ask for kiss, after kiss, after kiss;
such soft lips where such sugar-sweetness dwells,
as sweet as where lies the beehive's honey's cells;
her ravishing cheeks... so beautiful and so bright,
had stolen the full moon's radiant, glowing light;

her straight form the cypress-tree truly expresses,
and being full and ripe invites countless caresses;
yet, she, with all of these charms the heart to win,
still there was a kind of grieving, a torture within:
none could see or understand her grief… or heard
and walking, she drooped like broken-winged bird.
Her secret thoughts…her love she was concealing,
but often quietly to the terrace she was stealing…
from morning to evening she went gazing around,
in the hope that her Majnun might soon be found
wandering into her sight. Because she had no one
to sympathize with her plight: not one, not a one!
None to be compassionate, understand her woes…
she became afraid of rivals and of friends and foes:
and though she smiled… in her mind deep distress
began to fill her thoughts with a strong bitterness:
the fire of absence upon all her thoughts prayed…
but no light, no smoke… that fire in her betrayed
as she shut her lip from inside herself and she ate
and absorbed her grief from within, disconsolate;
yet, it's true… true love has many resources still,
it has also its soothing arts… and so it forever will!

Voices, quiet and guarded rose to where she stood
upon her balcony... listening as hard as she could:
she sometimes heard her faithful lover's suffering,
repeated in his songs... nearby they'd be singing.
The sky, with grey, gloomy clouds over it spread...
eventually, soft showers the clouds began to shed
and what, before, only dark destruction seemed...
with some rays of better promise, now, it gleamed.

Voices of the young and the old she could just hear
beneath high walls of that harem reciting her dear
Majnun's breath-taking songs; each thrilling word
heard, lifts her almost broken heart... every word!
Layla, that beauty with matchless, charming face,
had not only physical beauty... but mental grace:
with perfect eloquence and absolute taste refined;
and from those fine treasures of her gracious mind
she poured out her deep, warm love in a confession
with her faithful love's most intimate expression:
she let flow all of her dear hopes and sorrows over
and over, (although told a thousand times before);

the hot life-blood circling throughout all her veins
recorded on paper in songs her touching strains...
and as she wrote with passion flushed to its peak
in words of blushing-crimson, if they could speak!
Now she walks to the terrace and as she ascends
turns to see if she is seen, over the rampart bends
and flings that poetry from her heart with a sigh...
to a one who happens at that moment to pass by:
not seen by a soul that stranger gains that prize,
from that blessed spot away like lightning he flies
to where her lingering, faithful lover is weeping...
jumping to feet with surprise and happily crying,
he gazes, then listens, devours the pleasing tale,
then reads and joy again lights up his face, so pale.

In this way was resumed the exchange of thought
they could return their feelings as they'd sought:
both an intercourse, conspiracy in words pursued,
and so mutual vows more ardently were renewed;
and many the time between them went and came:
the dear moments of their love's deathless flame;
now with Heaven's hope, now in despair's abyss,

and now both are wrapped up in a visionary bliss.
That gloomy veil of night has finally withdrawn...
how sweet and refreshing looks the silvery dawn:
the rich blossoms shake and laugh upon each tree,
like those men who can face a fortunate destiny...
or perhaps the bright, happy face of joyful revelry.
And now crimson tulip and golden blooming rose
their sweetness to the whole world they disclose.
I, Nizami, look closely at shimmering pearly wave
and the fountain that the banks of emerald bathe;
the flocks of birds in every magnificent arbor sing,
and even the yellow-eyed raven hails this Spring;
presently the plump partridge and ring-dove raise
their joyous notes into the blue in songs of praise;
but the nightingales, through that mountain-vale,
like poor Majnun, chant only the mournful tale...

This new season of the rose has led Layla over to
her favorite bower and soft breezes blow through
and caress her cheeks of the softest vermilion: her
eyes are so much like that modest *sumbud* flower.
She has gone beyond her father's rich, painted hall,

she's gone from the terrace where she'd softly call
her lover's name where she'd stand alone... often
secretly watching, 'til night made the light soften,
and where she often stood and waited in suspense
until at midnight when she wept, losing all sense.
And now a narrow, golden ribbon sparkled around
her dark brow and it tightly her black hair bound;
and as on the green meadow she quickly walked...
a train of her beautiful girl-servants, ruby-lipped,
fresh of bloom like famous flowers of Samarkand,
obediently each of them bowed to her command.
She glowed and glittered like the full moon among
the young beautiful stars of that sparkling throng,
with forms as lovely as those Houris of paradise,
or Peris, angels in male form, with glancing eyes;
and now they finally reach an emerald water pool
hidden beside a secluded, unknown grotto, cool...
that peacefully was lying underneath that shade
and nearby a scented rose-bower had been made:
there in quiet conversations and sport and play...
minutes and hours not noticed swiftly pass away;
but sad Layla silently to the nightingale she tells

of that secret grief that her sweet bosom swells...
and imagines that through those rustling leaves,
she from the garden's soft fragrant breeze receives
the sweet secret breathings of her own true love,
as warm and as loving as the cooing of the dove.
In that romantic place in the garden where this all
happened, a grove of palms stood proud and tall:
never before in the Arabian desert's wild terrain
did a more enchanting view be seen and remain...
so exquisitely fragrant, and of such a rich colour,
not even Iram's fabled green pasture knew better;
no fountain ever existed half as clear and sweet,
as that which flowed at Layla's small... lovely feet.

It was there that grove of palms her steps invite...
and strolling its various outlooks give her delight:
its pleasant bushy thickets and those evergreens,
make her heart be aware of such pleasant scenes.
wherever a pleasantly scented soft breeze sighs...
there lilies and roses to see her by that breeze rise:
for some time all of the scenery charms her sight,
for awhile in her eyes and in her breast... a light!

But a nostalgic sadness then over her spirit steals,
and thoughts, too deep to hide, her state reveals:
beneath spreading cypress-tree she then reclined,
and in secret silent poetry she breathes her mind:
"O my dear faithful friend, and my lover so true...
you still remain far away from your Layla's view;
you are still absent, you are still beyond her power
to bring you to her waiting in her fragrant bower;
O brave and noble youth, are you still only mine...
and Layla... does Layla still only to you incline?"
And, as in this way, she almost in a dream spoke,
a voice that reproached her, her attention woke...
"What! Have you sent modesty from your mind?
and shall success be given to one who is unkind?
Majnun, on crashing waves of despair is tossed...
Layla, hasn't one of her luxuries or pleasures lost:
Majnun, has sorrow gnawing away at his heart...
Layla's indifferent looks different thoughts impart;
Majnun, the poisonous thorn of suffering endures,
Layla, with all her wiles and softness, still allures;
Majnun is her victim in a hundred thousand ways:
Layla laughing, in pleasant times spends her days;

Majnun's innumerable wounds all sleep destroy...
Layla keeps existing but in the fresh bowers of joy;
Majnun: always bound by love's mysterious spell,
Layla's bright cheeks cheerful feelings seem to tell;
Majnun... the absence of Layla forever he mourns,
Layla's carefree mind... to other objects it turns."
Because of this rebuke of her, tears began to flow
down Layla's face that now dejection does show;
but soon this blow to her glad heart was known...
her quick covering trick also practiced by her own
always waiting, playful servant-girls was seen by
them who kept watching: their eyes seeing a lie...
and they recognized in her voice of love and look,
that sign which never a woman's glance mistook.
And her mother too, with a much more keener eye,
she understood more deeply this deepest mystery,
but Layla thought her love story remained veiled
and often about her fatal choice of love she railed
but she, Layla, she still kept loving on... the root
had sprung up and now it bore both bud and fruit;
and continued in her belief that her secret flower
was as safe as a rich treasure in a guarded tower.

On that same day on which she thinking, strayed
out to the grove of palms... that day she walked
by as a sweetly blooming, young Arabian beauty,
she was followed by her girl-servants... all pretty!
Her moist red lips glistened, as her teeth of pearl,
her hair fell out loosely in many a bewitching curl;
and so it happened that upon that eventful day...
a fine youth with laughing friends came that way:
he suddenly saw that lamp of beauty gleaming...
he gazed on her lovely eye with softness beaming;
and immediately in his breast rose a kindling fire
of what soon became an increasing ardent desire.
There and then resolving her hand he would claim
(Ibn Salam was this fine youth's honoured name),
her from her parents... he would seek his success!
He went to them offering to tie the nuptial-knot...
and to help that joy scatters gold, more than a lot,
as if it were to him nothing but the common earth
or only sand, or water... something of little worth.
As he was of a high birth her parents found it hard
to believe him: a marriage they couldn't disregard;
and even though they consented, they still prayed

134

the nuptial morning might somehow be delayed
because, in her no ripened bloom could yet be seen,
that sweet pomegranate was still firm and green;
but they decided that she would upon a future day
have bridal yoke around her spotless neck to stay:
"We'll then surrender our virgin daughter to you...
Layla who until now was not promised, it is true!"
The promise soothes his young, enthusiastic heart,
and so pleased, he and his happy followers depart.

Majnun, out in that wilderness and that solitude,
his mood of deepest melancholy he again pursued;
in more serious moments of anger, loudly he raved,
into desert's burning noon bravely he often walked
or perhaps foolishly, and where dark shadows fell
were the same... as he sang of her he loved so well.

The Arab chieftain of that particular wild domain
who wandered here and there, trying to maintain
his seemingly endless terrain, was well respected
for his generosity and for helping those neglected.
Noufal was his name... well known for wielding

weapon to victory in battles beyond remembering:
his great glittering sword would often overthrow
those countless robber-bands or some martial foe;
he... no less than magnificent in pomp and state,
and he was just as wealthy as in his valour: great!
On this particular day, the pleasures of the chase
brought this incomparable chieftain to that place
where Majnun stood... then to him he came near,
not far from where he'd chased the bounding deer.
The stranger's face Noufal tried hard to recognize
and the sad notes of grief's song to hear; his eyes,
on completely seeing Majnun's mad expression,
closed as his ears heard that mournful confession.
Opening them... he saw that wasted frame there,
that head appeared to be all-overgrown with hair,
and that wild, wild look, which well might claim
brotherhood with despair... dejected, full of pain,
born by grief to life's last deep dark narrow abyss,
wounded feet, rags, singing this... of death's kiss.

Noufal had travelled over forest, copse, and glade,
seeking game: and here he found game that made

him wonder: game? A shade of a human he found:
but a one so light he scarcely touched the ground.
Dismounting straight away, he hears of the woes
which have tortured the poor youth's sad repose;
then he compassionately tries with gentle words
to show what innumerable pleasures life affords,
through this to prove the uselessness... the folly
of nursing sorrow, grief and morbid melancholy;
and even worse, when men from reason does flee,
and willingly steep their hearts in terrible misery.

Of course the natural sympathy of generous minds
around hearts of the suffering its influence winds,
and so, ever soothing, ever comforting by degrees
is restored its long-lost hope and quiet harmonies.
Majnun... who for so long to love had been a prey,
with death's swift decay coming quickly his way,
began to be influenced by that kind calming spell,
that sweet delight of which it's impossible to tell,
which can sometimes remove us out from our self:
and so now a change gradually came over himself;
with a trembling hand he slowly took up that cup

in Layla's name drank the life-restoring liquid up.
His spirits rose: now the refreshing food provided
at Noufal's overflowing hospitable table soon led
his mind away from his mood, his wandering off,
all he had to endure… at which people would scoff.
And then a delighted Noufal he gazed at a sight
so joyful it was hard to believe his own eyesight…
soon he hears him singing glowing songs of love,
while thinking of her he cooed like a turtle-dove.
Changed from who he was, his mind now at rest,
in the customary robes for relaxation he dressed;
an expensive turban, it shades his forehead pale,
and no more is heard the mad lover's frantic wail,
but now joking and cheerful as the vintner's guest,
he laughs and then he drinks with an added zest:
his prison of gloom has been exchanged for day…
his hollow, pale-yellow cheeks a rosy tint display;
he enjoys eating all of the garden's fruity sweets,
and afterwards his lip always the full cup meets;
but still he is devoted and unchanged is his flame,
never forgetting to inside be saying Layla's name.

In friendly conversations, heart uniting with heart,

Noufal and Majnun hand in hand are never apart,

away from each other they are unhappy to be seen

as they often walk by fountain in meadows green.

But what is such friendship to an intoxicated soul

that is accustomed to much more intense control?

A mere zephyr that goes… breathing over flowers,

compared to a fierce tempest… blowing for hours?

A soft zephyr's like the friendship's gentler course:

a tempest can compare to love's tumultuous force;

because a friendship leaves a kind of vacuum still:

which uncompromising love… love alone, can fill.

And so like this Majnun felt; and Noufal, he tried

without success, to fill that aching, growing void:

for, although the liquid that is sparkling and red

kept flowing, his friend full of sorrow finally said:

"My generous host, me with much you've blessed,

never of a foreboding do you think of… it is best!

Your great kindness many a help to me has given,

but not one solace comes my way under heaven…

you see, without my love, in tears I will languish,

and there is not a voice to check my deep anguish;

like one who is terribly thirsty and is about to die,

and every fountain that is to near him is bone dry:

thirst is by some water quenched, not by treasure,

nor by floods of wine and not by festive pleasure.

Bring me that cure that my wounds really require:

quench in my poor burning heart this raging fire;

only my Layla, O only my Layla give, Layla give

or your helpless friend... must soon cease to live!"

Majnun had only then his wish finally expressed,

when immediately, in generous Noufal's breast

there arose that firm resolve to serve his friend...

and to do so... Layla's unbending father he'd bend.

Afterwards, lifting high his keen Damascus blade,

he calls a band of his seasoned fighters to his aid.

As swift as the feathered race the assembled train

rush out, swords in hand, along that desert plain;

and when her chieftain father's habitation, bright

on the blue horizon strikes each horseman's sight,

he sends a messenger forward to claim the bride,

in terms commanding attention, not to be denied;

yet... that claim was still derided: "You will soon

repent of this foolish mistake: Layla is the moon;
and who the splendid moon can presume to gain?
Is there on the earth a man so mad, a man so vain?
Who draws their swords at such a hazard? None!
Who would strike his crystal vase upon a stone?"
Noufal once again tries to inspire fear even harder
with threats of vengeance at Layla's proud father;
but the threats are again useless, the same reply...
"Both your power and threat of vengeance I defy!"
The talking is over and Noufal draws his sword,
and with his horsemen pours down on that horde,
ready for battle. Spears and helmets loudly ring,
and brass shields: loud twangs of archer's string;
the field of conflict like the crashing ocean roars,
when the huge waves burst down on the shores.
Arrows, like birds, upon opposite foes stick out...
drinking with open beaks from each bloody spout!
The shining scimitars in the battle's raging heat...
rolled many heads under the horses bleeding feet;
and lightning... hurled by death's unsparing hand
spread consternation, through that weeping land.
Into the middle of those horrors of that fatal fight

suddenly... Majnun! A strange, appalling sight!
Wildly he raved, confounding friend and enemy...
his garments torn in a dreadful frenzy of misery;
then, with a mad stare full of reproach, he cried...
"Why fight like this when you all are on my side?"
The enemies all laughed, the uproar louder grew...
no pause the brazen drums or the trumpets knew;
strongest hearts sank at all death there gathered;
swords blushed to see all the heads they severed.
Noufal with a dragon's fierceness prowled around,
and he threw many a dying warrior to the ground:
whatever hero happened to catch his deadly mace
was crushed, even if firm as Mount Elbêrz's base.
Upon whatever head his bloodthirsty weapon fell,
there was always one heart-rending story to tell.
Like a rampaging mad elephant the enemy he met:
with hostile blood his blade continued to be wet;
wearied at length, both tribes at once withdrew,
resolved with morning the combat they'd renew;
but Noufal's brave friends had suffered the most;
one hour more and the battle had been surely lost;
and some more assistance by the following dawn,

from other friendly warrior tribes was then drawn.
And now the desert rang again... in front and rear
glittered bright sword and buckle and long spear;
again the struggle woke up the echoes all around,
swords clashed, blood again made red the ground;
book of life with dust and carnage was so stained,
that soon it was destroyed... not a leaf remained.
At last the tribe of Layla's father had to give way,
and Noufal had won the bitterly contested day...
a great many lay bleeding of the conquered band,
and died without any relief upon the burning sand.

And now the elders of that conquered tribe appear,
imploring the proud victor: "Hey, chieftain... hear!
The work of slaughter is complete and you see our
power all destroyed: wretchedly we all now cower
as the conquered do, begging at your merciful feet:
how many warriors faces, dusty plain now greet?
The scimitar and the spear have laid them all low;
see our kin lying silently, you're now without foe.
So pardon whatever wrong there might have been:
and let us leave this sad and sorry, bloody scene

unharmed... let us go, there is no reason to make

us stay and your prize, the Arabian maiden... take.

Then her father came forward, full of grief saying:

(ashes and dust upon his old head was laying)...

"Ah, no... with you how useless it is to contend!

You are the conqueror... and to you I'll now bend.

Without any resentment us the vanquished view,

the wounded and old and the broken-hearted too;

reproach has now fallen upon me and it has dared

to insult me, calling me Persian: that, I disregard,

for I'm still an Arab and scorn this cowardly sneer

of bragging fools, unused to the shield and spear.

But let it pass, because now I, overcome and weak,

and prostrating, pardon from you the victor seek...

I am your slave and I'm now obedient to your will,

lay here ready your most difficult purpose to fulfil:

but if I consent with my daughter Layla to part...

will you remove all the vengeance from your heart?

Speak immediately to me, what you want declare:

I'll not flinch... though in two it my soul may tear.

My daughter shall be brought at your command...

let the red flames flare up from the blazing brand,

awaiting their helpless victim, crackling in the air,

and Layla doing her duty shall surely perish there.

Or if you would rather see my dear daughter bleed,

then let this thirsty sword do that dreadful deed...

Cut off with one blow, my daughter's lovely head,

Layla's sinless blood by her father should be shed!

In all things you shall find me to be faithful, true,

your obedient slave, what would you have me do?

But take notice of me now: I am not to be beguiled;

I will never to some demon give my precious child:

I will never, never to that madman's wild embrace

give the greatest pride and the honour of my race,

and have her wed to contempt and foul disgrace...

I will not sacrifice our tribe's proud name and fame

and never smear with disgrace her virtuous name.

Is honour nothing? Better beaten by a bitter fate...

than to yield our honour, even for a king's estate.

Throughout all of Arabia her virtue is well known;

her beauty is matched by heavenly charms alone.

I'd prefer in some monster to be forever enshrined

than bear a name that became hated by mankind.

What! Wed a wretch and earn my country's scorn!
A dog's better than a man of a mad-demon spawn.
A dog's bite heals, but such a human's bite, never;
the festering poison-wounds will remain for ever."
This was what the father said. In Noufal's breast
feelings were aroused... no longer to be repressed:
"I had hoped to win your consent to this," he said,
"But now that anxious hope I had is totally dead,
and you and your companions may quit the field,
still armed with the lance and sword and shield...
all of your horsemen and old men. And so, in vain
a rain of blood has rained upon this thirsty plain."

When Majnun this final speech of Noufal hears...
he flies incensed towards Noufal, and with tears
he wildly cries: "At dawn, O my generous friend,
you promised me this day in happiness would end;
but you have now let the lovely gazelle slip away,
and you've defrauded me out of my beautiful prey!
Near where Forát's fair stream rolls on, I reclined,
bathing wounds, hope soothed my tortured mind,
and you gave me Layla; now that hope is crossed,

and life's most valued gift is gone... forever lost."
Noufal, with a heavy heart, now homeward bent
his way and Majnun with him sorrowing went...
and there again hard that pitying chieftain strove
to calm the withering pangs of this hopeless love;
to bless with his gentleness and with tender care,
Majnun's wounded spirit, sinking deep in despair:
but his efforts were useless; mountains and plain
soon heard this madman's screaming cries again;
escaping from listening ear and the watchful eye,
once again alone... to desert wilderness he did fly.

And now the minstrel strums softly upon his *tar*...
with the sound, full of foreboding all listening are;
as the balmy air's filled with his mournful playing
he continues his sad tale... as he begins singing...

That melancholic bird who'd been made to cower,
from day to day in Noufal's garden's dark bower,
had tired of the scene, so with a first ray of light,
then swift as the desert wind he had taken flight,
and now... far from Noufal's wide, wild domain,

he has his freedom in another wilderness again...

pouring out to desert and hills his sad complaint,

in the wildest of moods without care or restrain.

And now far away from all people and any town,

amongst the tangled forest... parched and brown,

the mad horseman roams... with a double speed,

he furiously goads along his large, snorting steed,

until soon in a quiet, green grove, a hunter's snare

attracts his eyes... struggling to quickly get there,

its sharp knotted meshes have held tight between

them an imprisoned deer, a sad sight he has seen;

and, as that nearby hunter suddenly to it springs

to grab it and then, as he the deer promptly brings

towards his knife that is now lying upon its neck,

his eager hand receives a sudden, powerful check;

and then he, looking upwards with much surprise,

(a mounted chieftain's son, there before his eyes!)

He stops, and now the youth begins his pleading:

"If your chest with a little compassion is beating...

don't do that! Because it is a terrible crime to spill

the blood of a gazelle, it is boding nothing but ill;

now listen...please set that pleading captive free:

sweet is all of life and everything deserves liberty.
That heart of a one must be as hard as the marble,
as merciless as the wolf or as the panther terrible,
that'll cloud with death that enormous dark eye,
that beams brightly like Layla's... O so lovingly.
That cruel deadly stroke, my friend, please hold...
that creature's fine neck deserves a string of gold.
Look carefully at its slender limbs and at the grace
and heart-entrancing meekness of its sweet face.
That pod, the musk it holds is its fatal attraction,
as beauty still is the prey of a powerful ambition;
and it is only for that fragrant gift that you're led
this gentle, trusting gazelle's blood to now shed!
Hunter, please do not seek to gain by a cruel deed,
listen to me... don't let an innocent victim bleed."
"But," cried the hunter, "these gazelles' are mine;
I can't give up this work... from this task resign...
it is the hunter's work and it is free from all blame,
to watch and to snare some of this forest-game."
With this, Majnun, alighting from his steed, said:
"Let it live! Forget them, take this steed instead."
The hunter rose, eagerly taking the Arabian steed,

and... laughing, rode from there at a great speed. Majnun, delighted, looked at his purchased prize, and in the gazelle's eyes he sees his Layla's eyes: "Ah, so like Layla, don't fear for I am your friend even if this wild look you see in me may offend... O so like Layla, if you would only stay for awhile perhaps for a moment my face could again smile." But soon, freed from that snare, with nimble feet trembling, it headed for another more safe retreat. Majnun is startled and he finds, being amazed... the vision has vanished which his help had raised. "Once I'd untied her she quickly went on her way never knowing but for Layla she'd be dead today."

The dawn of the new day spread its radiant light between the spokes of the sky's wheel of night... while the awakening sun painted a fresh red rose upon the horizon... like a flower in Autumn arose Majnun... so beaten down by grief and exhaustion his head drooped and when the sun towards noon shot arrows at him... he was overjoyed to discover a small oasis where under palm trees spring water

invited him to drink... then rest in that cool shade.
Majnun thought: 'A piece of Paradise, this glade
has fallen to earth... it is an image of the grounds
that Paradise's lake, named Kauther, surrounds.'
Having drunk until full he lay down on the grass
in the palm's shade to rest... and let the sun pass.
Exhausted, in peaceful sleep, time passed quickly:
sun was low in the west when he woke suddenly,
feeling that someone at him had been staring...
But who? No living soul far, near, he was seeing!
He happened to look up at the top of the palm, in
whose shade and protection he had been resting.
There... in the crossed greenery of the fan-shaped
branches he saw a shadow: a large raven squatted
and stared at Majnun, his eyes glowing like fires.
Majnun thought: 'Dressed in mourning, he also is
a wanderer... in our hearts we must feel the same.
He yelled: "Blackcoat, who do you mourn? Came
in the colour of the night in the light of day... oiy?
Are your eyes burning in my grief's fire and have I
a companion for my soul with your black shroud?"
When the raven heard Majnun calling out so loud

it hopped on another branch without ever taking its yellow eyes off Majnun who went on shouting: "If you, like me, belong to those whose hearts have been burnt, why shun me? Are you dark and grave like a preacher... ready to preach from your pulpit: or a black watchman... if so, why in fear still sit? Listen closely to me now... if, while flying, you see Layla, the one whom I love... tell her this from me: "Help... please come and help me in my loneliness, for my lonely light's now fading in the wilderness. 'Majnun, don't fear, for I am yours,' you had said, please do not hesitate... or you could find me dead. If caught by the wolf the lamb will hear all too late the shepherd's flute that laments its terrible fate. Dying from thirst, I keep searching the sky in vain but... too late will be the cloud bringing your rain." As Majnun finished this poem... the raven hopped further and further away... until it finally fluttered from the top of the palm tree... and into the fading light which seemed to swallow it up... kept flying. It was no longer day... but as yet it was not night: the hour when the bats wake up... and take flight.

Soon the night became as black as a raven's jacket:

a great raven of a night... a night as black as jet!

After those wings were stretched out they reached

across the sky and yellow raven eyes again stared

down on Majnun like before, only now there were

countless numbers of them, unlike the pair earlier.

To escape from their gaze, Majnun covers his face

with his hands... weeping bitterly, fills that place.

When the morning light shone through the curtain

of night the old world came alive... a new garden!

Majnun could not stay away from her any longer:

nothing could stop him from feeling love's hunger,

he flew along as if he had grown a raven's wing...

or like a moth rushing to the flame to be burning.

The nearer he came to his goal, the more his heart

became drunk with what Layla's scent did impart;

the louder his ears did hear the sound of her voice,

her face he saw in the landscape and did rejoice!

All strength left his limbs, he had to have a rest...

he was like a man who for long had been a guest

among the dead... and now with his every breath

and sigh, feels life returning as if from near death!
While resting he saw two odd figures approached,
a woman dragged a man... hair, beard disheveled,
his limbs were chained... he almost couldn't walk;
he behaved strangely, talking a kind of mad-talk:
the woman was pulling constantly on the chain...
hurrying him like an ox or beast without a brain.
Majnun was shocked, felt pity for the poor beggar
and implored the woman not to abuse her prisoner
so much and asked: "Who is this man... and what
has he done to pull him around tied up like that?"
"Do you want the truth?" Asked the old woman.
"All right... he is neither a criminal nor a madman.
I'm a poor widow and he is 'God's fool', a dervish,
and we have suffered great hardship and anguish:
we're ready to do anything to fill purse and belly,
and that is why he is in these chains like you see,
we hope people will think he is mad and give to us
food and alms... we divide the spoils between us."
Majnun went down on his knees and begged her...
time and again he went on with begging of her...
"Relieve him of his chains and put them upon me,

for I am one of those with a disturbed mind... see, I should be tied up, not him! Take me with you as long as you want... all given to us will be yours." The woman didn't hesitate, she quickly unchained the dervish... Majnun was soon heavily chained. It was as if she had given him a great gift and she walked on leading her new victim smiling happily. When the woman and her prisoner came to a tent, they stopped: Majnun sang his poems, then went limp, crying: "Layla, Layla," and banged his head and body on the rocks and then she pulled and led him by his chains as he danced around like a fool, then... she knocked him down for them to ridicule. One day they came to an oasis by a stream where some tents were erected as they came closer there came a sudden recognition... it was Layla's tent! Tears began to stream from his eyes like a rivulet pouring from Spring's dark clouds. He collapsed, and hit his head upon the ground as he shouted... "You left me to myself... sharing with me nothing but your grief! See, I am doing penance... suffering because I made you and yours suffer under Noufal

and as a punishment I am shackled like an animal.
I am here to be chastised, knowing I've committed
a sin so great it can't be forgiven." Then he said...
"I'm your prisoner, you're my judge... condemn me!
Punish me however you like, because it's obviously
my fault that your people suffered and now I keep
beating my body with both hands... while I weep!
Yesterday I committed my crime, today I am here
in chains to suffer any torture from you, you hear?
Kill me... but please don't reject me in my misery.
Could I... plead innocence before you? Not really!
You're loyal, even when loyalty you've abandoned!
I'm guilty even when by innocence I have been led.
While I was alive, you didn't send greetings to me,
and your hands did not stroke my hair... lovingly.
But now... there is the hope that perhaps you will
look at me while with your arrow, me you will kill.
Then will you finally place your hand on my head?
Perhaps you'll draw out your sharp sword instead:
let me lay my head like an animal to be sacrificed?
I'm Ismael before Abraham, I wait to be sacrificed!

Why should I fear if it's you who cuts off my head
for my heart's like a candle... if the wick's gutted
it burns even brighter! As long as I am alive every
way is blocked that can lead me to you... you see?
So save yourself from me and save myself from me
and let me rest at your feet in eternal tranquility."
Majnun could say nothing else, so with a wild cry
he shot off like an arrow... his face insanely awry.
Shouting, as if possessed by a demon, he grabbed
his chains and with unbelievable strength spread
them apart and breaking them... striking his face:
from the old woman and Layla's tent he did race.
Away from human beings he ran and ran and ran...
to Najd's wild mountain... from man and woman.
His parents, his relatives and friends now heard...
they knew about his exploits but this was absurd!
Some relatives searched... but when he was found
in his mountain hideout, they saw that the ground
of the past apart from Layla's name and memory,
had fallen from his mind: only Layla he could see!
As soon as they attempted to talk about anything
else he became silent, or he escaped, withdrawing

into himself... as if he was intoxicated with sleep.
These attempts excited him... he'd begin to weep
but this led nowhere... in the end even his father
and mother abandon all hope, he may ever recover.

It's night and the darkness as black as Layla's hair
veils everything... and his soul is oppressed there;
no bright moon like Layla's face to him appears...
no glimpse of light Majnun's dark outlook cheers:
now, inside an old cave black with despair he lies,
the tedious moments marked... only with his sighs.

Look... and see the great clouds of dust now there
way off on the lonely desert's far horizon... where
on high the far sky by whirling dust is covered...
the azure colour of heaven is completely obscured.
And now the loud tramp of flying steeds is heard,
and now is heard the leader's shouted angry word,
now much nearer and more distinct they all grow:
who is that angry, shouting leader, a friend or foe?
No! It's Layla's recently vanquished proud father,
he is riding home with his heart on fire with anger

for though he and his men have survived the blow,
still burning in him the disgrace of his overthrow.
His tale is now told to all... some demon or ghoul
had so obviously paralyzed his own fearless soul,
and held back his powerful arm by a magic trick...
or potion from a witch's bowl stirred by a lunatic;
or he would've driven all evil, with an easy hand,
along with the miscreant Noufal from this land;
for when was it that a proud and a powerful lord
failed? Only when evil magic... did stop his sword!

While he tells his tale, shielded by harem's screen,
his daughter Layla, sweet narcissus, can be seen:
with her eyes downcast she listens, disconsolate,
to her father's bragging words that seal her fate;
and what is it that poor Layla now has to bear...
but only loneliness and reproach and deep despair,
with no congenial spirit as it was before to impart
one single comforting word to her breaking heart!
Meanwhile, spicy-smelling breezes from each side
are sending much praising of her beauty's pride

through neighbouring tribes, and in more remote places her name is whispered... her favor is sought.

Suitors with various claims appear... those great, those rich, those powerful... they impatient wait to hear for whom that father is keeping that rare and fragile crystal, watching her with all his care. Her charms they eclipse all those others of her sex given to be loved... and a rival's heart they'd vex; for when the lamp of joy illuminates her cheeks... the lover smiles, and yet his heart it surely breaks: and so the full-blown rose sheds its scent around; but there are thorns not charmed that also wound. Among others come courting that stripling came... the one who had before declared his love's flame; his happy, confident, countenance seemed to say that for him was certainly fixed the nuptial-day. His countless offerings... they are so magnificent: splendidly embroidered garments to win consent... and the richest, the rarest of gems one could hold, and many carpets worked with silk and with gold: amber and incomparable pearls, and rubies bright;

and now enormous bags of musk attract the sight,
and the best, well-fed camels of unequalled speed,
and some ambling, old and fine... of purest breed:
he rests for awhile, and then all of his gifts sends
off before him... with instructions to his friends,
to fathom all their eloquence and all their power...
to be persuasive to bring to him the favoring hour,
to magnify to her father his worth, and also prove
that he and he alone is deserving to have her love.
"A youth of royal presence... he of Yemen's boast,
fierce as a the fiercest lion and powerful as a host;
of untold wealth, with utmost bravery he wields
his conquering sword in all the best battle fields.
You call for blood? It'll be shed by his own hand.
You now call for gold? He scatters it, like sand."
And when flowers of speech their scent had shed,
diffusing highest honors around the suitor's head;
exalting him to more than any a mortal's worth...
in person 'manly' they express, 'noble in his birth';
the sire of Layla seemed oppressed with thought,
as if with some repulsive feeling his mind fought;
yet immediately the answer was given... he soon

decreed the fate of Yemen's splendid young moon

by saddling steed of his own want... he, in truth,

flung his own offspring into the dragon's mouth.

So, very soon the nuptial pomp and the nuptial rite

engage that chieftain's household... and every site

rings with banging of drums whose noise goes far

and, a greater clamor is heard through the bazaar.

The pipe and the big cymbal, so shrill and so loud,

delight all there in that joyous assembled crowd;

and all are laughing happily and join the festivity,

with songs and wild dancing, enjoying the revelry.

But all the time Layla always mournful, sits apart,

the shafts of dark misery stab through her heart...

and some black and portentous cloud could hence

be seen darkening her normal outward appearance:

her breast swells again... again with heavy sighs,

now tears gush out of those heart-winning eyes...

where Love's triumphant sorcery... and magic lies.

In the midst of blooming Spring like withered leaf

she droops in the terrible agony of unending grief;

loving her love... loving Majnun, and him alone;

everything else from her affections now has gone;

and soon to be joined, in but a moment's breath...
to another! Death! No... a fate worse than death!

As soon as the sparkling stars of the fateful night
had finally disappeared, and great floods of light
came out from the morning sun's glorious beam
colouring in purple the Euphrates rolling stream,
the bridegroom, joyous, arose to inspect... to see
if the bride was equipped as his bride should be...
the litter was waiting and also the golden throne,
prepared for his blessed bride to rest herself upon:
but what is the use of the utmost of tender care...
and the fondest love, when deepest, dark despair
and complete and utter hatred fills the fair breast
of that one to whom that fondness is addressed?
Quickly, her sharp contempt the bridegroom feels,
and from her scornful presence shrinks and reels...
a solemn oath she then takes and to him she cries,
with a frenzy of madness flashing from her eyes...
"Did you have the hope that I'd be yours one day?
It is my father's will, not mine! This, to you I say:
than to be a thing that by me would be abhorred,

all my life's blood I'd prefer to lose by your sword.

So, away with you! Do not any longer seek to gain

a heart that is forever doomed to an endless pain...

a heart, that no power you may possess can move;

a bleeding heart that scorns you... and your love!"

When Ibn Salám... her frenzied look his eyes held

and heard her vows, all his hopes were dispelled.

He soon perceived what craft had been employed,

and his bright visions were faded and destroyed;

and he found, when love turns a maiden's brain,

father and mother urge with their power... in vain.

All of those Arab poets who rehearse and rehearse

their immortal legends in such imperishable verse,

say that when Majnun these tidings finally knew,

much wilder and more mad, more erratic he grew;

raving through the woods and the mountain glen;

running still further away, from all haunts of men.

All of a sudden a perfume, so grateful to his soul,

over all his awakened senses very quickly stole.

He thought from Layla's fragrant couch it came,

and it filled with joy his poor, exhausted frame.
And now, ecstatic with the unexpected pleasure,
the fondest memory of his most dearest treasure,
he sank upon the ground... and beneath the shade
of a broad palm tree, in a senseless state he laid.
And then a stranger, who was quickly passing by,
observed that poor, lovesick, young wanderer lie
sleeping... or dead, and he slowed his camel's pace
to try to recognize the features of his crazed face.
Loudly shouting... roaring like a demon, he awoke
the madman from his trance and laughing, spoke:
"Up, up, get up you lazy-bones! Up! Understand
what desire of your heart has done for you... and
it's better to drive all your feeling from your mind,
as there is no reason to have faith in womankind:
it is so much better to be idle, than to be employed
in such a fruitless toil; listen to me: better to avoid
a mistress even though of form divine she may be:
even if she is as beautiful and false as yours! See...
they have handed her over to another, also young:
the bridal-veil now over her brow has been hung...
close, side by side, from morning until late night,

kissing and making love has become their delight;

while you from human companionship stay away,

and from love not returned you die more each day.

Being far away from the sight of who adorers her,

only one in a thousand might be true: you concur?

The pen that continues to write, it is as if it knew

that a woman's promise will always split in two.

While she is cradled in another's warm embrace...

not being able to see your condition... a disgrace,

without any faith, on you she wastes no thought,

because she is wrapped in her own faith... naught!

A woman's desire is far greater, also more intense

than a man's, and much more exquisite her sense;

but... never to be completely blinded by her flame,

her gain and fruition of her plan are her final aim,

the love of a woman is a selfish love... that is all;

possessions, wealth... are security to stop her fall.

How many a false woman and cruel women prove

this, and not one of them was faithful in her love!

Her life's nothing but a contradiction! Yes, her life

is peaceful on the inside and within it is all strife!

Yes, a dangerous friend indeed and also a fatal foe,

the prime breeder of a world of suffering and woe.
When we are experiencing happiness… she is sad;
when we are immersed in melancholy, she is glad.
And so, this is the kind of life that a woman leads,
and with her wiles and sorcery she still succeeds."
These hate-filled words confused the lover's brain;
fires of despair ran though his every swelling vein:
frantically, he smashed his forehead on the ground,
and blood came trickling from the ghastly wound.
"What added curse, is this?" Groaning, he said…
"Another tempest, now roars around in my head!"

Was there ever a time when lover's bleeding heart
didn't betray his love with reason's sickening art.
Can the most skilful of talented gardeners always
keep his flowers or his fruit in each season's days?
O no… hearts that are dissolved in grief give birth
inevitably to madness… just as this teeming earth
will always yield herbs… and yet bewildered mind,
that to all but one bright object seems to be blind,
never suffers any kind of criticism from that seer
who guides the faithful Muslim population here.

Love sanctifies the thinking that may be mistaken,
and Heaven will forgive deeds by madness taken.

Majnun spoke as if alone: "A lovely rose, I found,
with many thorns and briers circling all around...
and, struggling to possess that rose... that prize,
the frustrated gardener those sharp thorns denies.
Look at my heart, it is all torn and it is bleeding...
in the pangs of pain all others they are exceeding...
I am seeing all the leaves expand and then bloom,
I am smelling that rose's most exquisite perfume;
its color I am witnessing as it blushes in the light,
gives to my soul that is in rapture, unique delight:
I go and am weeping beneath the tall cypress-tree,
and nothing happens... still the rose is not for me.
Ah no! It is hopeless! No one listens to my moan:
that pride of my soul, my beautiful rose... is gone!
And now another has gone in the open light of day
and taken that heart-winning prize of mine away.
Although she was wrapped in sweetest innocence,
that cruel oppressor took her away with violence.
But who really deserves all the curses that are said

and thrown upon the disgusting betrayer's head?
Her father, *that* gardener, in his lust for more gold,
that perfect rose, the boast of all of Iram, he sold.
Poor wretch: if worlds of wealth were mine to give,
without any hesitation all of them to him I'd give;
but not one *dirham* would I ever give for that rose,
which seems to be the fatal cause of all my woes.
I would never play that loathsome villain's part...
and buy with gold and treasures a woman's heart;
it is never possible with gold to buy another's love,
love is above all wealth, and any price it is above...
because... I would much rather be dead than to see
a smile that is on any lips that are not really free.
Give to me only the boundless swell of true bliss,
the heart that is freely springing up to the kiss...
when one's life and one's soul and breath combine
to tell me that she who I only love... is only mine,
with the flood of joy completely overwhelming all
my glowing senses... with a delight beyond recall.
Contemptible wretch! You, you who the rose sold:
the worst curse of any demon be upon your gold."

The traveller had witnessed with growing surprise
how this mad heart had suffered before his eyes...
Now... he wondered what remedy could he offer?
Then from his camel leapt that shocked traveller;
when the sufferer seemed to be almost restored...
begging forgiveness to him he anxiously implored:
"I was wrong, and *I* completely deserve the blame;
I spoke lies and with those lies defamed her name:
my mistake is of the darkest that there could be...
my crime's the worst... Layla's still true, you see?
Listen, though with nuptial band she was united...
still her faith to you that by that one was slighted
remains without blemish, still firm and unbroken,
as proved by many a mournful refusal, unspoken.
And it is true... space of every moment can claim
a thousand, thousand recollections of your name:
and so you're there... ever present in her memory,
she still lives, but now only lives for you, you see?
One year has passed since she was made a bride;
but what of years? Whatever time may provide...
even if it were a thousand, her heart is the same,
unchanged... as is still her cherished first flame."

Majnun, still desolate... his fate he now could see
as if viewed in a glass, his state of abject misery:
for from the first conversation he'd heard no relief,
he still felt alone and lost with no end to his grief.
Like a sick bird he fluttered while his lay his head
down and on looking to that magic point that led
to where his angel-faced Layla was forced to stay,
in a voice full of melancholy he whispered her way:
"Ah no! My passion glowed in me... in every part;
you on your tongue, but never really in your heart;
with your new love have you now in love grown?
Am I always to be as worthless as a desert-stone?
What is a word, a promise, an oath... or a pledge?
Only a mockery, that in the heart is only a wedge.
What was my garden's wealth: fruit and flowers?
And all that wealth I had... a raven now devours;
and what has been all my constant care and toil,
to have another come and spoil the nurtured soil?
When at first... to be yours, my soul was destined,
I thought little... about that treasure I'd consigned;
think of your broken vows and what they require:
worry about the lies: think of its end, a quagmire.

My doom is fixed; I've no more freedom to choose;
this martyr's life is yours, I have nothing to lose!"

Meanwhile, his father mourned his own sad state,
like Jacob cried over his Joseph's unknown fate...
no rest came to him by day and no sleep at night,
grief over his old body shed its withering blight;
incessant chasms of sorrow opened in his heart...
as he sat in darkness, silent, from all others apart,
he whispered: "Why, from home, did my child go?
Where's my poor wanderer gone? I need to know!"
He dreaded that the relentless scimitar of death...
had taken from the one he loved his final breath.
Suddenly he rose, despair had given a little vigor
to his old body... and as if in some kind of fever,
and almost frantic with remorse and with shame,
and now gathering upon himself all of the blame
he travelled through the forests and desert wild,
seeking to find once again his poor, forsaken child;
and when the day ended... withdrawing its light,
in a cold, rough cave he passed the dreadful night,
but not thinking of anything other than his quest,

no peace for him came and no strengthening rest.
Without any success the desert he looked around,
but not a single trace or word of him was found...
until when a Bedouin herdsman crossed his way,
and he told of the spot where he knew Majnun lay.
Craggy and deep and terrible for his eyes to view,
it seemed like a grave... damp with a noxious dew.
He climbed down and was by that herdsman led...
where in horror he discovered that grave-like bed;
fearing of the worst... he suddenly sees the wreck
of his once lovely boy... a serpent round his neck,
but, like a pet...it stays awhile where all around
it lies half-devoured limbs... bones on the ground.
With cautious descending steps he slowly surveys
his unconscious son, who meets his anxious gaze
on waking with a wild look that cannot recognize
the tottering old form before him: "Who are you?
And why are you here?" He replies... "Don't you
know me? I'm your father! I have found you now,
after a long search!" Embracing, both show how
deeply confused and upset they are and when he,
the mad son, has eventually regained his memory,

and beams of light burst through his upset brain,
and looked harder and knew his father once again,
joy sparkled in his faded, clouded eyes for awhile,
and his parched lips seemed to curl into a smile.
His poor old father whispered in his weak voice...
"You make my old feeble heart tremble and rejoice:
that path over which you feet are doomed to pass
has swords blades, not harmless blades of grass,
and I must warn you that you never should roam:
your only safety now is to come and stay at home.
Dogs have a home and you have none, it appears:
are you a man that at any human comfort sneers?
If you're a man, then like a man you should appear,
or, if you're a demon, be a demon right now, here!
The ghoul, that was created to confuse this earth
is still only a ghoul and is answerable to its birth;
but you, you're a man; and why, with human soul,
do you forget your true nature... become a ghoul?
Today, if you should be throwing the reins aside...
tomorrow you may come and ask... and be denied.
Soon, I shall surely pass away and I will be at rest,

and no longer be this frail world's unhappy guest.

My day is mingling with the shades of the night...

and my life is now losing all its life and its light.

O soul of your father! Inspired again with grace...

rise... protect the honors of your family, your race!

So that, even if this frame be in the grave laid low,

I may at least the guardian of my birthright know;

so that even if I die... to stop an old parent's grief,

you may be hailed in your own home, as the chief.

Heaven forbid that when my last hour has passed,

my house and home to the winds should be cast!

That plundering strangers, with a rapacious hand,

should waste my treasure and spoil all of my land!

And Heaven forbid, that both at once should fall,

(my greatest dread): in that way extinguish it all!

That when the summons finally reaches me to die,

my son's death should also swell the funeral cry!"

These words sank into Majnun's heart: he seemed

altered in mood... as through his senses streamed

the memory of his far-off home and his love for his

dear mother and the joys he shared... and her kiss

and her love. For many days and nights he'd tried
to banish from all his thoughts that other's bride:
he'd repent of that... and then repent of *that* too,
that tyrant, love, *that* feeling would soon subdue;
(love, that wild and mighty elephant which grows
more powerful... when opposed by friends or foes);
and that poor madman to his father finally said...
"Your counsel father, is the wisest, best ever said,
and I'd like nothing but to your wish to conform...
but... what am I? A helpless wretch, only a worm,
without the power to do whatever *I* may approve:
I am merely a slave... the victim of almighty love.
To me, all the world is swallowed up and I can see
nothing but Layla... everything else is lost to me
except for her image: my father, mother and home,
they are all now buried in an impenetrable gloom
beyond my feelings... and yet I know you are here
and I could weep... but what's the use of any tear,
even if the one tear was at a father's funeral shed?
It's known... human sorrows never reach the dead.
You say... that the night of death is on you falling:
then I will weep, your paternal care I am recalling;

but I... I shall surely die alone and in utter misery,
and no one shall be left... who will weep for me."
Then old, weak Syed Omri, with unutterable grief,
gazed upon his son, whose sorrows mocked relief;
and, hopeless, wretched... every thought resigned
that once was balm and comfort to his poor mind.
And then showering blessings over his son's head,
groaning, away from that dank chasm he was led,
and anguished, to home his camel's head he gave,
but as he'd expected... he went home to his grave.
Gently he slowly sank, by age and grief oppressed,
from this world of illusions to that of endless rest.
A world of illusions indeed! Who ever rested here?
Look, the illuminated moon has its eternal sphere,
but all mankind... who in this mortal prison sighs,
appears like lightning... like lightning, away flies.

Much later, and a pilgrim reached the wild retreat
where Majnun still lingered upon his rocky seat...
the sad tale of his father's death was told. He fell
upon that inhospitable ground, almost insensible;
and groveling... frantically screaming into the air,

he beat his chest until bleeding and tore his hair...
and he never rested, not in the night or in the day,
until, grieving, he had after wandering far away...
at last came to the lonely spot where at peace lay
his father's bones... crumbling away with decay.
He dropped... his arms around the grave he flung,
and to the dusty ground deliriously he now clung;
grasping at that dust that was covering the dead,
he madly threw it over his lowered, shaking head,
and with the countless, repentant tears he cried...
where holy relics had been laid by that graveside.
And now, overwhelming was the sharpened sense
of his sorrow and repentance... deep and intense;
and a sickness had taken over his shattered frame
in a slow fever... parching lips with a great flame;
still... without break he continued to loudly mourn
upon his father's sacred grave from night to morn:
he felt deep inside his heart the bitterness of fate;
he saw his foolish mistake now but much too late;
and many a world he would give... again to share
his dear generous father's constant love and care;
for he realized that he had often without thinking,

condemned the wise and the old ones counseling;
and how he had with a child's impatience burned,
and how he had scorned any sympathy returned...
and now like all those beings of the human mould,
when the indulgent heart of anyone becomes cold,
which would have stopped forever his happiness...
he begins to mourn... but mourns his own distress
for... when that diamond blazed like brightest day
he had thrown it all stupidly and recklessly away.

Who is that one wandering near that palm glade...
where a fresh breeze adds coolness to that shade?
It is Majnun! He has finally left his father's tomb,
again upon rocks and on scorching plains to roam,
he takes no notice of the sun's fierce midday heat
or the damp of the dewy night, with his bare feet;
he never gives a thought to forest's savage brood,
that howl on all sides in search of meat and blood;
he fears nothing that is from the earth or the air...
from den or eyrie: he remains calm within despair:
he seems to court new perils and can contemplate
with unflinching detachment scenes of dark hate;

and yet, still he is gentle and his gracious manner
checks extended claws, where blood does gather;
for the tiger, wolf and the panther, now lie around
Majnun as king... licking his hand and the ground;
the fox and also hyena their fierce snarling cease,
the lion and the fawn lie down together in peace...
the vulture and the soaring eagle, up on the wing,
around his place of rest their flying shadows fling:
like Solomon, over all of the creatures is his reign;
at night his pillow is the lion's shaggy, soft mane;
the clever leopard on herbage himself does spread,
and he forms like a rich man's rug a romantic bed:
and together the lynx and wolf in harmony stay
while running over the field, playing all the day!
All of them pay homage with a respect profound
as they, enchanted... circle him round and around.
Among all of the others, one of the little fawns ran
with nimble skinny legs as fast as a new fawn can
and... in one beautiful leap that was so delicate...
sprang to where the admiring Majnun sat in wait:
so soft it was, so meek it was... and sweetly mild,
and so shy it was, so innocent, yet it was so wild,

and it was so playful... as it was held in his sight,
and the more he saw the greater his great delight:
with his eyes he loved its pleasing form to trace...
and he loved to kiss its full black eyes and its face
so sweet and that made him think of Layla more...
the heart will take any reflection to itself restore;
and with the illusive dream once more impressed,
he hugged his favorite of all animals to his breast:
and then, with his loving hand that fawn he fed...
those choicest of nearby herbs before it he spread;
and all beasts that had come and assembled there
each one on his own receive his most loving care...
and by day and night each of them unconstrained,
in a wonderful harmony... together they remained:
and so it is, throughout this whole world, we find
among the animals, as well as among humankind
a helping hand and sometimes the friendly voice,
that tells to the most savage of hearts... to rejoice.

Listen... there is a curious story that has been told
about a king and a despotic ruler... in days of old,
a story that some ferocious beasts were endowed

with a deep sense of gratitude... this, was proved!

The dictatorial king had inside his palace's bounds

a den of vicious, man-eating, enormous hounds...

and everyone on whom his unrestrained anger fell

were arrested, then thrown into that dreadful cell.

Among the nervous, old courtiers there was one...

who for wisdom, wit and shrewdness was known,

for a time in the royal household he was nursed...

but this courtier, he was always fearing the worst,

always thinking... that fatal day might soon come

for himself to be sharing that same horrific doom;

and so... by devising an extremely clever scheme,

his life if he needed to, he endeavoured to redeem.

So, unseen he went during night, and often stood

and he fed all of the hounds with a savoury food;

and so well their bountiful friend they now knew,

and in each mastiff's heart... an attachment grew;

then, when just as he, prophetically had thought,

the cruel king his death without thought, sought;

with a stern look his good old courtier he blamed,

to the ravenous dogs to be thrown he condemned.

It was late at night when into the den he did cast

his poor, innocent victim for those dogs' repast:
the next morning, being unashamed by his deed...
(dooming to death an innocent victim... to bleed),
he called and sent his den-keeper to look at him...
torn, he confidently expected... from limb to limb:
the den-keeper who was curious, and who obeyed
the king... and not for a second was he delayed...
now hurrying back into the king's presence, cried,
"O king! Believe me, his innocence has been tried;
this courtier, he carries an angel's blessed charm,
and God, obviously protects his life from harm...
untouched, although still chained, I did find him,
and the dogs were... fondly fawning around him!"
The cruel king was struck with great amazement
at this totally unprecedented, miraculous event...
and going and himself seeing, in that horrid cell,
that guiltless, old courtier safe and looking well,
he asked, after he had many tears profusely shed,
by what strange spell that courtier was not dead?
"Not a magical, juggling word did I have to say...
all I did was... I fed these bloodhounds every day;
it was because of this... that their gratitude arose,

which has saved me from you, the cruelest of foes.
I have been faithfully serving you for many a year,
and for all my service you have sent me down here!
A dog has some feeling, but you... you have none!
A dog... a dog is always thankful, if given a bone;
but you, you with blood covering both your hands:
O no! No spark of gratitude: who, understands?"
Shocked and ashamed that despot saw his crimes,
changing the course of his cruel life... for all times.

Sweet slumber diffused the blessed charm of rest
through the mad-lover Majnun's agitated breast
and as the magnificent morning, clear and bright,
poured over the cloudless sky its deep purple light,
waking up... out of the right side of bed that day,
he rose... refreshed, and hailed that heavenly ray.
Graceful... he stood among those of various herd,
and, warmed with hope, his songs they preferred;
when suddenly a horseman riding fast he did see,
who, obviously... this mad lover knew, instantly!
"O you, romantic young man! I see that timid deer

and that fierce lion that meet in friendship here...
and you the monarch... strange! Listen, I declare
a secret tale of one, who is so loved, who is so fair.
What would you feel, if I... did her name, declare?
What worth is cypress... to her form that is divine?
What's that perfume coming from martyr's shrine?
Her ringlets twist like the graceful letter 'J'... *Jim,*
her shape is an 'I'... *Alif* ... mouth: 'M', a *Mim;*
her two eyes are like those narcissus... that grow
where pure spray of many fountains slowly flow...
her fine eyebrows joined by a double arch express,
her beautiful cheeks that any angel might caress.
But what can *I* of such absolute perfections... say?
What can I... to a blind Creation's charms... say?
I saw her weep... those tear-drops, glistening, fell
in showers from eyes which their own tale can tell;
and yet, I asked for whom she wept and mourned
for one who is untrue or one who to dust returned?
Opening her unforgettable ruby lips she then said:
'My heart is covered with salt and all joy has fled,
once... I was Layla... need I, more to you reveal?
Far more than a thousand madmen, is how I feel:

more wild than the dark star that rules my fate...
more mad than my Majnun... is my insane state.
And if that dark spirit you should happen to find...
that... that terrible wreck of a enlightened mind...
how will you recognize him, that one? By his sad
disordered features... so often pronounced as mad;
or... by that unutterable grief which always preys
upon his heart... producing that melancholy gaze,
which has no sense of outward things... that love
so pure... it's like it's some emanation from above.
O... if only I could escape from this... from it all...
and leave... forever leave my father... leave it all!
Now go and seek my wanderer in desert and cave
patiently explore and find his refuge, or his grave:
find him; and, faithfully, with your unwearied feet
return... immediately, tell me his forlorn retreat.'
Without speaking, I listened to her earnest prayer;
I listened closely to her despondent voice and air...
and while she... still, in the most tender of mood,
with tears flowing from her eyes, before me stood,
the story of your desperate troubles... which long
had been your theme and others of many a song,

now familiar to everyone, all the country around,

and these I sang, and then a deep affection found;

so deep, that many sighs, succeeding many a sigh,

she let out... as she trembled in her terrible agony,

and, then senseless, Layla sank upon that ground,

where suddenly pale... totally motionless she lay

as if her life had... instantaneously... flown away.

But as soon as that dreadful swoon was finished,

and many sobs and tears her heart had relieved...

again she begged me to restore him she adored...

'If you're kind... and you must be to one abhorred,

I feel that you would never play the traitor's part;

you can't disdain my misery... my breaking heart.

Ah... no! Although I may seem to that one untrue,

pity still remains to be given... as a woman's due.'

Her beautiful, long, nimble fingers then did press

the written evidence... the story of her distress...

then raising this tearful letter to her ruby mouth,

this desperate and passionate record of her truth,

she then kissed it at least a thousand times... shed

a flood of tears, while mournfully she softly said:

'To him and only to him... this sad memorial give,

for him, for him alone I live... for only him I live!' "
Majnun, perplexed and by painful feelings driven,
seemed to refuse what still to him was... Heaven;
many imagined falsehoods swept across his mind,
but still... left no dark distrustful thoughts behind.
And then finally her written letter eagerly he took;
but as he read it he faltered, then wept and shook.
Adoring the Almighty Creator like this she began:
"Beyond all praises of the tongue of a mortal man
is His love and His goodness," her writing went:
"He... with light of wisdom, to the soul joy sent;
he orders the cheek to glow and the eye to roll...
and every mortal alive is bending to His control.
To this, He scatters jewels so bright and so rare,
to that the good sense to strive with worldly care:
to me He gave this love which all of time defies...
the spotless love I bear you from beyond the skies;
the fountain of Khizer that sparkles in the shade!
The fountain of life to... your own Arabian maid!
In truth and in love... to you my heart was given,
that truth and love remain... the gift of Heaven.
Though far from you, now a wife against my will,

I am yours... I promised... I am your partner still:
I still remain single and still pure and full of faith,
unchanged, I am yours... unchangeable in death.
You are all of the world to me... and the very earth
that you walk upon is to me of matchless worth...
and yet it's in this different sphere my race is run,
I'm the moon and you my love, are the radiant sun:
in this way, by destiny kept apart, how then can I
be criticized... who at your feet would gladly die?
Since we're in this way divided please pity my lot,
because all your vows and raptures I never forgot;
my life's sweetest flowers in their brightest bloom
turned into bitterness of that devil-tree of doom!"

Then Majnun... wept bitterly and shook; and now
what answer could he possibly frame... and how?
He a wanderer, completely destitute with no reed,
with no piece of paper that would supply his need:
ah... but Layla's faithful messenger had brought
the means: in this way the distraught lover wrote,
"To that One Who formed the great starry throne
of the heavens... He, Who rules the world alone;

that One Who in the dark and mysterious mine...

makes all of the precious, unseen diamonds shine;

that One Who also on human beings life bestows

being the gem that in devotion grows and glows...

to that Almighty One be all gratitude and praise,

and remain the theme of Muslim poetry, always!

A burning heart like mine that lies in grief so deep,

what can it continue to do, but to sigh and weep?

And what can this writing on a piece of paper bear

to you, but the wailing of one in deepest despair?

I'm nothing but the dust beneath your perfect feet,

although you, I am destined never again to meet.

Your incomparable beauty's my Kaaba, my shrine:

the arc spanning the heavens: you're forever mine;

you're my Garden of Iram, but... hidden from me,

you are the Paradise that I am not allowed to see;

and yet... you've snuffed out my hope's last light;

my day... has now become like the blackest night.

With only great affection on your flattering tongue

you smile my way... my heart in despair is wrung;

for those whose tongues are gentlest to be found...

are often the ones delivering the deadliest wound.

The petals of the white lily... so often they appear

to be as fatal as sharpest sword or longest spear.

That one, whom to me it was a rapture to behold,

could that one so fine be basely bought and sold?

Your promise to me, could you that promise break,

and turn away from me... for some other's sake...

could you play a cold and callous deceiver's part,

and then go off and be a solace to another's heart?

But, give peace! No more of such thoughts so sad,

or I shall surely become even more intensely mad...

I am longing no more those precious lips to press...

but is the ecstatic joy of remembering them... less?

The morning's breeze your fragrance to me brings,

and now suddenly my exulted heart for you sings;

and still yet more when upon reflecting I can see...

that one time you graciously, filled the cup for me.

O... Heaven on Earth! How rapturous to receive

that which is forbidding my heavy heart to grieve,

to sit with you all day and in love's way to play...

and be quaffing the ruby every day in every way:

to kiss those delicious lips... wet with honey-dew,

of liquid bright... and of cornelian's clear red hue

O... if only I could see and kiss them once again!
This fantasy lights a fire in my bewildered brain.
I'd need the art of the painter... to be able to trace
those perfectly drawn lines... of your angelic face!
Ah... yes! All of them are now indelibly impressed
for all time inside my ever-faithful, beating breast.
And so... it is now our divided destiny to deplore
that those scenes we can never witness anymore;
but, although on this earth we are denied to rest,
shall we not both in Heaven... be forever blessed?"

Among Majnun's relatives was a one whose kind
heart had won the approval of those of like-mind.
His name was Selim Amiri and Majnun's mother
was his sister... and she knew this modest brother
had always loved his nephew, trying to kindly see
a way to help but had failed... he'd felt the misery
of his nephew's sufferings from far off. He would
try to ease his misery... sending clothes and food.
Now, he felt it was time... Majnun he would see!
Who knows... perhaps there was still a possibility
that wandering nephew would finally come home.

But he must trace his steps, to where did he roam?
Mounted on his steed swift as the wind, one day
he sought the distant place where Majnun lay...
and eventually him, with a peaceful face he found
with herds of wild beasts: him, they did surround.
Frightened of their savage natures he soon retired,
until Majnun, calling, confidence in him inspired.
"Who are you, what do you want?" Majnun cried
"I am Selim, from the tribe of Amir," he replied
"I'm one also with whom fate has played, but you
must know that! I am your uncle who loves you!"
Only now did Majnun know his guest, so then he
ordered his animals to stay back and immediately
asked him of his family, friends... about himself.
Selim was surprised by Majnun's mental health:
this is a 'madman', deserving of the name given?
If judged only by his looks the name's well-chosen!
But... as he examined his sister's son more closely
Selim felt shame and grief in his heart... and pity.
Why is this? Majnun was like a naked corpse that
should at least be covered... he would see to that!
To that corpse without a coffin, ashamed, he said:

"Let these robes shade your naked body and head,
these robes I brought here... for you." "Not for me!
I want no covering, without clothes I feel I'm free.
Look at these tattered fragments, thrown aside...
these once were robes, and once my foolish pride."
But, pressed by Selim again, those robes he put on,
and he sat like death... like his dark, doomed son.
Now savoury meat-stuffs were before him spread,
but not one morsel of them he raised to his head...
he turned around... and scorning that fine repast,
to his wild, animal friends all of the banquet cast.
Then Selim asked: "What's *your* food, my friend?
Without any food your life will soon quickly end!"
"The freshness of my spirit... and its secret power,
is from breeze that begins morning's opening hour:
yes, every soft breeze from my dear beloved brings
life to this soul of mine... upon its fragrant wings;
and when hunger presses, from the weeping trees
I gather gums, the hunger's cravings to appease...
and herbs and grasses and waters from the creek
keep me in this state you see me... I'm not weak;
but, although the offered food doesn't interest me,

all the beasts are now enjoying it as you can see...
and if I decided that on some living thing I'd feed,
birds I could easily catch... but, I detest that deed;
and one who herbs and grass is contented to eat,
defies the whole world... the world lies at his feet;
for... what can pomp and wealth and feasts avail?
I live upon grass... now listen to that Zahid's tale:
in those times of long, long ago... a king, they say,
through wild, forbidding forests went on his way
and suddenly slowed... then he pointed as he rode
towards a reclusive Zahid's desolate, old abode...
he asked a number of his attendants if they knew
what the recluse's habits were... what did he do:
to find out what was his food, and where he slept,
and why remote from all the world this man kept?
Immediately an attendant towards the Zahid ran,
and he was soon bringing forward that holy man:
"And now tell me... why do you pass all your days
shunning the world's inviting, captivating ways...
and why'd you choose this dismal, wretched hole
that seems like a grave... for both body and soul?"
"I have not a single friend to love me, not a one...

and nothing is in my power, except to live alone."

There, where his fawns were, them he quietly fed,

giving them some blades of grass... then he said:

"This, is my food... only of this I need supplies!"

The king's attendant looked with scornful eyes...

then he finally answered: "Taste some royal food,

and you will never again believe grass is so good."

"Indeed," the Zahid said... then he slowly smiled,

"that... is a sad mistake, my poor, hopeless child!

Those still of this world are still to luxury prone...

to you, sweetness of this simple food is unknown:

you are obviously a stranger to such delicious fare,

no doubt you are partial to food much more rare!"

Soon as this Zahid's answer that monarch heard,

noting, with much attention, every single word...

as he wondered at his luck at such a seer to meet,

he fell and prostrated at that pious Zahid's feet,

and the king kissed the green grass while he knelt

outside there... where the contented hermit dwelt."

Over Majnun's spirit, for so long in darkness cast,

a glimmer of a homesick feeling suddenly passed;

so now he asks Selim of friends he once preferred,
and asks about his mother, a broken-winged bird;
and he wishes perhaps even to visit home again...
as if that maddening fire had finally left his brain.
Selim, with reason glimpsed, grasped opportunity
and... to his mother's distant mansion he quickly
took the wanderer, where deeper became her grief
to see how withered had become that verdant leaf
and how the rose had faded from his young cheek,
and his eyes so changed... his thin body so weak:
from head to foot she kisses him, and then weeps:
his matted hair she seeps in her tears... and keeps
clasping him lovingly... tight to her beating heart,
as if she would never from her body let him part...
"My darling boy! The game of love you've played
has... in its way... you to a mere shadow reduced;
in that sad affair on which I'll not waste a breath,
you grasped that double-edged scimitar of death.
Your father has gone and his troubles are all past,
poor, heartbroken man! And I? I shall follow fast!
Take your true place and enter your mansion here,
knowing it is your own home... now doubly dear:

your nest... birds although distant in their flight,
always return to their own nests when it is night.
While you were still an infant in your cradle-bed...
I watched you slumber, pillowing your sweet head;
and can you, now that your mother's love you see,
be unmoved by how big her love for you must be?
Can you refuse the joy your presence can impart,
and cast yet another shadow over her poor heart?"
A cloud again obscured the sunny light of day...
and once again his wavering mind he gave away:
"Mother, there is no hope for the time is now past;
with an eternal gloom my fate has been overcast;
it's no fault of mine, no crime pressing me down...
but, my countless sorrows to you are well known;
like a poor bird that within its cage is imprisoned,
my soul... has too long this prisoner's life endured.
O dear Mother... don't ask me to remain at home;
because here, to me no peace can ever truly come.
Much better it will be for me to continue to stay
among those mountains, with my beasts of prey,
than to continue to linger here where human care
that makes stronger all my misery and despair."

He stopped, then kissed his mother's feet and fled
immediately towards the dangerous path that led
to the wild mountains. So sudden was the stroke!
Majnun's mother's heart like his father's... broke;
and so in death's cold ocean, wave followed wave;
a short time later she followed him into the grave.
Once again, Selim the madman's haunts explored,
with a mournful voice the tragic tale he revealed...
both his old father and his dear mother were gone,
now... there was only himself, left terribly alone,
sole heir: doom sealed, beating brows... from eyes
fell tears of blood and his haunting, piercing cries
rang through the forest and mountains and again
pouring out the saddest, wild cry without restrain,
and then he suddenly ran from that gloomy cave,
to moan and weep upon his mother's recent grave.
But eventually when that sudden outburst of grief,
that terrible agony was so intense, but, still brief...
and in the end he was left alone in a milder mood
to love Layla... he walked his mountain-solitude.
To him, what was their name, their hoarded store?
The wealth of his parents for him existed no more!

Hadn't he not so long ago, this mad, ill-fated one,
abandoned everything... all for love, for love alone?

Meanwhile, Layla hearing all his poems, had seen
what Majnun's deepest feelings had always been;
and though her faith in everything seemed broken,
she held his words inside, love's tenderest token:
but even so, deep inside her heart a thousand woes
disturbed all of her days and all her nights repose:
it seemed that there was a serpent at its very core,
that writhed and gnawed in her more and more...
and there was no relief in sight: a prisoner's room
was the cold womb of that lovely sufferer's doom.

Fate at last looked towards her with a favoring eye
on a black night... with no watchmen walking by;
eventually she had luckily reached the outer gate,
where shrouded and unseen she sat down to wait,
eyes flashing to each side, praying to quickly find
some friend to help her to calm her troubled mind;
when into her sight came an answer to her quest...
a holy seer towards her came... her prayer blessed,

he was that one who always, like an angel, strove

to the bitter anguish in depth of the heart remove;

the holy seer lived only to succour the distressed,

to soothe and staunch the bleeding, broken breast:

to him she spoke, whispering: "For pity sake hear,

one wretched... one distraught with love and fear!

Do you know the youth, that one of peerless grace,

who stays far from here in a secluded wild place...

amongst animals savage or tame and fills the air,

crying... 'Ah no... for me there is only despair!' "

"Ah yes, lovely moon," he answered, "well I know

that unlucky wanderer and his ever cureless woe;

Layla is still always on his tongue, the Arab maid

he ceaseless seeks through every bower and glade,

unconscious of the world... its bloom or its blight,

Layla is all there is that is remaining in his sight."

The Arab maiden wept, and cried... "O, no more!

I am her... the cause, and I forever his loss deplore;

we both have our sorrows, both are doomed to feel

the deep wounds of absence that will never heal...

for me he roams through wild desert... while I fear

fate condemns me to be always confined in here!"

Then... from her ear a shining gem she withdrew,

which, having kissed, she it to that hermit threw,

and said... "Forbid that I should ask you in vain!

Please let these loving eyes see his dear face again,

but, caution must control the zeal your eyes show:

some signal by you must be given, so I may know

when he is nearby, perhaps some lines of his own

sung beneath my windowsill, where always alone,

I sit and I wait and I watch: for secret must we be,

or all will become lost to my Majnun, and to me!"

Within the belt around his waist the smiling saint

put the magnificent gem... on his errand he went.

But was there not an obstacle his task did oppose?

Daily thousands of obstacles to his mission arose:

wherever his arduous course he anxiously urged...

perplexing paths in various lines always diverged;

through groves, the ground with creepers spread,

and meshes of shadowy branches fell on his head,

now a wide plain stretched, then mountains grey,

now an emerald-green meadow cheered his way...

and then at long last, on a small hill's shady side,

the sought for love-sick wanderer he finally spied
surrounded by many beasts of the forest, in a ring
like guards, appointed to protect their noble king.
Majnun perceived him and with an upraised hand
made his wild followers at a short distance stand;
and then the seer approached, his homage paid…
"O you, O you unmatched in love," he kindly said,
"Layla, that beauty of the world… beauty's queen,
who, for such a long time… adoring you has been;
and many a lonely year it is that has run its race…
it is long since she has seen your thoughtful face…
since she has heard the sound of your sweet voice,
which always made her heart cry out and rejoice:
and now, at her urgent command, I faithfully bear
her desperately pleading, her almost dying prayer.
She is longing to see you… at least one time again,
to secretly sit with you, soothe your heart's pain…
and once again feel, on pleasure's angel's wings…
the happiness that only a lover's presence brings.
And will you not, with equal happiness, with her,
set yourself free from all these restrictions forever?
The Grove of Palms your feet must quietly trace,

not far away from Layla's other dwelling-place.
That's the promised spot; and when you get there
you will receive from her pledge and vow... where
you must sing, with your voice subdued and clear,
your poem sweet and soft... into her waiting ear."
Majnun jumped up and with a look of happiness,
with the seer as guide they made quick progress
travelling as fast as possible that space between,
arriving full of optimism at that romantic scene...
where the majestic, swaying palm-trees displayed
a cool and refreshing depth of welcoming shade...
and there, those animal tribes of forest and plain,
which did form that wanderer's travelling train...
as promptly as would servants... a human retinue,
all to a nearby thicket of bushes quietly withdrew.
That old seer then advanced with a cautious pace,
to the secluded pavilion of Layla, that angel-face,
that star of beauty... and that sweet silvery moon,
and he whispered of the presence, of her Majnun.
A woman's mind can sometimes become strange...
and seem to change, without the power to change;
and because of this, she said... "No! It cannot be:

I must not meet him again... this is Fate's decree:
the lamp lit like this, Love's temple to shine upon,
will not enlighten but in the heart burn on and on;
for I'm now married, to another I have been given
(although worthless dust) in the view of Heaven;
although I was forced... let others bear the blame!
I was not born to sacrifice my good name or fame.
Prudence forbids that such a peril should be mine;
better to let me suffer here and to my fate resign...
but remaining faithful: with his melodious tongue
how often have sweetest echoes to me been rung?
Yes, still staying faithful, he may now into my ear
chant those glorious couplets that I love to hear:
let him with that pure nectar fill his luscious cup,
and... still adoring my love I will drink it... all up."

Prostrated, tears gushing, upon a fountain's side...
the old seer found Majnun who impatiently cried:
"What is this amber incense around me blowing...
is it the Spring's breath over the rosebuds sighing?
It is not that sweet fragrance of the early Spring...
only Layla's fine long curls, such a fragrance fling!

205

So powerful these impulsive feelings they impart,
that they fill with such ecstasy the lover's heart."
The old seer, well-taught in love's mysterious lore,
knew what it would mean to him that she no more
would come, said... "You can't now hope that she,
without you seeking, or you asking... you will see!
Woman always demands that her lover will show
his desire: away, her sacred power don't make go."

"Don't reproach me... not with some old saying,
and do you think that Majnun's desire is dying,
when, from the very scent upon the breeze, I feel
the intoxication of love... so totally over me steal?
Must the never-ending bliss of love never be mine,
must this lover never taste that luscious wine?"
After saying this while seated in that palm-grove,
to Layla he then began to chant his poem of love:
"O... where have you gone, where have you gone...
and where am I? Where am I? Alone... I'm alone!
I have been forsaken, I'm lost... and what remains?
Only life is remaining, creeping through my veins;
and yet that life-blood is really no longer my own,

but is yours forever... and I only breathe, to moan:
a thing only to be remembered... that came before,
sometime in the past, where hope smiles no more.
Being so familiar to the feelings which scorn relief,
grief smiles upon me... and I... I smile upon grief.
Grief makes you still more dear... for grief and you
seem born of each other. Grief paints for me, you:
your matchless beauty: without grief, no thought
of all your perfections to my mind is ever brought.
Heaven will never allow us to be doomed to part!
We are but one within two bodies, with one heart.
Like Summer clouds with rain the meadows greet,
Majnun dissolves in sorrow at your gracious feet;
while your soft cheeks lend beauty to all the sky,
Majnun... poor Majnun is taught by them, to die.
The nightingale over your roses joyously swoops;
Majnun, separated from you, weeps and droops...
and while the world devotes itself to more strife,
Majnun would instantly sacrifice to you his life.
O if only a kind fortune would our joys approve...
and yield to us the blessings of a successful love!
The gorgeous moon... with her translucent light,

converting into a dazzling day the darkest night;
and us... finally... together... seated... ear to ear,
the sparkling wine is our beverage, it's lying near;
I... playing with your long ringlets, which descend
in magic curls... and over your fair shoulders bend;
you... with those dark, those love-enflaming eyes,
in which the living spell of all magical sorcery lies,
gazing with your love upon me. That... sweet lip!
I watch it... as it the fine wine does lovingly sip...
I see us both... ah what love, ah what happiness!
None to drive away sovereign rights of a caress,
nor shame, nor fear, to crush love's bright flower,
as happy... we stay together in that secret bower.
Ah! Now bring me wine, this bright illusion stay!
Wine! Bring wine... to keep all sad realities away!
Wine, Winebringer, wine! A house without a light
is only a prison that is always odious to the sight;
because broken hearts shut up in gloom like mine,
are dark as dungeon, not blessed by light or wine;
O God... please save me from this endless night!
Give me one day of joy... one moment of delight!"
Then strangely moved, he quickly closed his poem,

sprung to his feet and then ran off again to roam;
and Layla, who had heard him... deeply mourned,
and sorrowfully, to her secluded home... returned.

Through many towns and campsites had spread
the story of love's madman and all anxiously read
it or heard it in Baghdad and more distant plains,
the mournful lover's poems... his pain's refrains;
and every other lover's heart that had been wrung
with frustrated love's lost hopes, in pity all hung
low... from those sorrows which to madness drove
mad lover Majnun... into that martyrdom of love.
And all of those sad lovers desired to seek the cave
which on any day might become his lonely grave...
to find that one who survives such grief... to view
that prodigy of love's torture... but seen by so few,
of whom the world in astonishment now spoke...
as being crushed beneath misfortune's heavy yoke
and whose truth and constant loving her excelled
all that other lovers in this world, had ever beheld.
And now, a gallant youth who for long had known
the pain of love, climbed onto his camel and alone

he impatiently searched... trying to be first to see
the mad lover now most famous for love's misery;
so many a mile across inhospitable terrain he rode,
before he reached the lover's wild, secluded abode.
Majnun could see him as he approached from afar,
and quickly sent his animal-vassals to their lair...
and then gave a welcoming wave, asked his name,
and asked from where the hurrying stranger came.
"I come, my friend, to make your heart again glad;
I've journeyed all the way from beautiful Baghdad.
In that far-off enchanting place it seemed I might
have lived in ecstasy and delight, day and night;
but, then I listened to your tender songs for days,
your sorrows of separation, that the world amaze;
and all that is only remaining for me on this earth
is to stay here with you... nothing else has worth.
Your poetic songs, your *ghazals* such joy impart...
that each word has become a treasure in my heart:
in love, just like you, I also often weep and I sigh...
so now let us together live and together, we'll die!"

Astonished from this young man's strange desire,
laughing, the mad lover answers, his eyes on fire:
"Sir knight! Listen! One so soon of pleasure tires?
And do you all your worldly pomp really despise...
all that your parents wealth, and luxury can give,
throw it away, so you with me in a cave can live?
Such a mistaken young man! What do you know
of those with a broken heart? What can you show
of a love like mine? Have you foregone the benign
joys of life and of every hope haven't a single sign?
Yes... I have companions, through night and day,
but they are inmates of the wilds... beasts of prey;
yet I do not ask for any other... I am needing none;
you see I would much rather live with them alone.
What have you from your high society seen in me,
when even hideous demons from my presence flee,
would you be able to brave the noon's great heat...
while you're unsheltered, naked from head to feet,
and the constant dangers of the cold midnight air,
to be with one like me... one not worth your care,
not worth one thought? Beneath this scorching sun
I wander the wilderness and when the day is done,

exhausted, I lay myself down on a beggar's throne
with my canopy the trees, my pillow a hard stone.
Houseless and poor and often faint with hunger...
how could I ever for a guest take in any stranger?
While you, surrounded by all your friends at home,
moved by no need at all, but by a whim to roam...
may pass your happy hours, laughing and cheerful
and never think of me... a wretch who is pitiful!"
The young man now placed before Majnun's sight
refreshments he hoped would tempt his appetite...
sweet cakes and fruit and from his basket he drew,
heart-easing wine... he was trying to get through
to him... to win the favor of the moonstruck man;
it was then his brief but his earnest speech began:
"Friend, please kindly share my meal and do allow
a small, joyful smile to clear your furrowed brow!
In bread there is life... for it strengthens every part:
while strengthening... it cheers a drooping heart."
Majnun replied: "The argument is true... it is just,
for without refreshment a man descends to dust...
nerve, power, strength from nourishment proceed;
but it is not the kind of nourishment that *I* need."

His reply... "Mortals change, whatever their aim;
nothing on this earth will ever remain the same...
understand, that you'll not be forever unchanged,
perpetual change the heavens above have proved...
and night becoming morning prove that it is true
you have loved, but freedom may yet come to you:
the heavens seem to be clothed in deepest gloom;
black like the night is the threatening day of doom:
but, the clouds fly off when the storm has passed,
and no longer comes howls of the scattering blast;
the heavens will then resume their brilliant sheen,
and much brighter will glow all this varied scene:
so... grief will always devour the heart for awhile,
so... one's frowns are always followed by a smile:
like you, I was enchanted... yes, I also was bound,
tied by love's bitter chains... around and around;
but to the winds all of my grief I eventually flung
and to my desperate fate I no longer tightly clung!
Ah... this fire of love that seems to burn so bright
what is it really... nothing but a treacherous light.
Yes... for a young man like you when it is all over,
those mountainous flames can hurt you? Never!"

Majnun, spurning such treacherous thought, said:
"You're speaking to me as if feeling in me is dead?
I am the one who is the king of love; and now glory
in love's dominion... and you would now have me
go away, abandon everything the fate of Heaven
has in all my suffering, for my solace to me given,
to quit that cherished hope... than life more dear,
which rivets me to the earth... and keeps me here?
That pure... that ethereal love, that mystic flower,
nurtured in Heaven and fit for an angel's dower?
What? To out of my heart expel the dream of love?
Listen, first from an ocean's bed the sands remove!
Useless is all your efforts and useless is your aim,
you cannot ever quench love's never-dying flame.
So stop this persuasion. Why to me do you appear
to be like a master, teaching, like some holy seer?
That one who tries to open locked doors, they say,
for him to be successful first must know the way."
Finally, the young man saw his error and did stay
there as Majnun talked to him for one more day;
and by the oracle of love chained by hopeless love,
he listened enraptured, to his many songs of love:

a companionship he found exquisite! Then he rose
to say goodbye because he could no longer impose
on the man of many woes... sadly he went away,
leaving him... surrounded, by those beasts of prey.

How beautifully blue the firmament! How bright
the moon is sailing across that expanse tonight...
and at this lovely hour lonely Layla quietly weeps
inside her prison-tower and her sad record keeps...
how many days, years, her sorrows she has borne:
an age of sighs and tears... a night with no morn;
yet in that guarded tower she lays down her head,
kept tightly inside like a gem within its stony bed.
And who's the warder of that place of many sighs?
Her husband the watch at day and night supplies!
What words are those coming to her anxious ear?
Unusual sounds, unusual sights at night appear...
lamps ghostly flickering and wailing sad and low,
seem to proclaim the sudden burst of another woe.
Beneath her window comes a call... a wild lament,
death throes disturb the night, and the air is rent
with voices calling for help but all hope has fled...

he breathes not... her husband, Ibn Salim is dead!
The raging fever quickly nipped him in his bloom...
he sank without love, without pity, into the tomb.
Layla sees the moon... a cloud stains its lucid face;
sad sign of a shroud, the grave their resting-place:
end of humble and proud! Now to her it is all told,
both the hands and heart of her husband are cold...
must she now be in mourning for the death of one
whom she had always loathed, to even look upon?
Clothed as is the custom, grief must be displayed:
wild hair, eyes red and a heart properly disguised,
she seemed completely distracted in her manner...
as if her heart felt a blow, from an inside hammer:
but all those burning tears that she profusely shed
were for her Majnun, and not that one, now dead!
That rose welcoming the purple glow of morning...
glistening anew with a balmy dew from it falling,
looked even more lonely when the cruel thorn had
been removed from where it grew... and more sad!
But the laws of Arabian lands still had their claim
on the pure widow: destroying a chance of blame.
For two years she had to suffer behind the screen...

for two years she saw no one and she wasn't seen:
no, not one glance in all of that long, lonely time,
as unseen she bloomed into life's luxurious prime
was allowed, to love's fine example of womankind;
she now to all but household faces had to be blind,
and she in her home her secret vigils had to keep...
as she had to be seen to be in mourning... to weep.
And Layla kept weeping, but who could really tell
what was the secret... that in her heart did dwell?
Those beautiful dark eyes in tears are swimming:
her heart may ache, but not for him is throbbing...
not for him who in the grave, unconscious sleeps:
it is only for beloved Majnun... that Layla weeps!
All day whispering the poetry of her distant lover,
a spell to charm, bless, soothe a heart's high fever.

"O what a night! O what a long and dreary night!
It is not night, but darkness without end in sight...
it's the extinction of an ethereal light without end,
without companion I sit... without a single friend.
Is that immortal source of light forever concealed?
Or is the dreadful day of judgment now revealed?

Nature's form is beneath a pall and cannot bloom;
O, what a night this is... of soul-destroying gloom!
Can the shrill awakener of each morning be dead?
Has the muezzin forgotten his call... still in bed?
Has that warder from his watch-tower run away,
or, weary of his task, returned to dust... to stay?
O my God! Please restore to me that joyous light
which first illuminated my heart... the pure sight
of young love... so in here tonight I no longer stay
and may escape to feel the bliss of a shining day!"

Years, months and days, how slowly they roll on...
and yet how quickly it is that life is going... gone!
Ah yes... the future too soon will become the past,
because the course of time is ceaseless. But at last
morning came, the king of day arose in fine array,
and Layla's dark night, had finally passed away
with morning... her morning of beauty on her face
shining... it resumed its beauty and sublime grace;
and then with soft steps of some angel's lightness
she moved: a glittering moon in its full brightness.
And now inside her... what was her greatest aim?

The impulse quivering inside her desperate frame?
Her secret love that she had for so long concealed,
now without a blush or fear she openly revealed...
at first she had called to herself her faithful Zayd
tried and true, she knew in him she could confide:
"Today's not a day of hope only false hope giving,
it is the day of real hope, a lover's day of meeting!
Wake up... because today, this world is full of joy:
get up and serve your mistress... you faithful boy;
'Where cypress grows near red tulip and the rose...
long separated lovers meet...' a note to him, goes!"

They met... but what to say? That heart deprived
of joy for so long knows it alone to have survived:
intense feelings had checked their power to speak,
a silent confusion sat down on each lover's cheek;
speechless with a love impossible in words... they
stood there gazing in each other's eyes all the day.
It is so that when a chamber holds no golden store,
no lock is needed to protect the always open door;
but when fabulous hoards of gold become the lure,
a strong lock is placed to keep that wealth secure;

so, when the heart's full, the voice is tightly bound
for an easy conversation with grief is rarely found.
Layla, with looks of love, was the first who caught
hold of the quiet expression of bursting thought...
"Ah... no," she whispered, as over him she hung...
"what wondrous grief's this, chaining the tongue?
The nightingale, famed for his sweet flowing note,
without the rose can still swell his tuneful throat,
and when in the fragrant bowers the rose he sees,
he begins to warble ever sweeter, in his ecstasies.
You're the nightingale of the garden's fragrant air
and I'm the rose... why not now your love declare?
Why, when I was absent, so long unseen by you...
up to heaven rose your voice and your poetry too?
And now after so long when we're together, alone,
your love has vanished... and your voice is gone?"
A great flow of tears to Majnun finally gave relief
and words came: "Misery is mine, mine the grief;
the memory of your lips, so balmy and so sweet...
tied my tongue, which would their charms repeat.
When I like a falcon, through the woodlands flew,
the slow, spotted partridge never met my view...

and now, when I'm here and unequal to the flight,
the long-sought beautiful bird comes into sight...
you are the reality, with angelic charms you show,
and what am I? I don't know... perhaps a shadow:
without you I am nothing. Desire would enthrone
us both together... melting forever into only One;
and in this way... united to each other forever, we
are equal... always equal in our loving constancy:
two bodies with one heart... and spirit the same,
two candles with only one, pure, celestial flame...
of same essence formed... together forever joined,
two drops in one and each soul to each resigned."
He paused... and then, with ineffable pure delight
Layla gazed on his countenance... and on it a light
long hidden from her sight... did its divine dance.
Now his heart is throbbing from her loving glance:
the fragrance of her curls surrounding her smooth
perfect neck, her jasmine-scented breath to soothe
him and her sweet confession of trembling eyes...
that ardent love which all time and chance defies,
the chin of dimpled sweetness and the soft cheek,
those open ruby lips that were preparing to speak,

maddened his finest feelings... and so once again
a sudden tempest rushes madly through his brain:
crazily gazing furiously around himself for awhile
he looks at Layla with a strange, a ghastly smile:
then as he tears off his garment in a frantic mood,
he turns, as if with more than a man has endured,
and shouting he hurries off into the desert's plain,
followed by his beasts... in a strange animal train.
His love was as chaste and as pure as all heaven...
by too much separation to madness he was driven,
a vision of divine rapture filled his searching soul
and... his sublime mind hated any kind of control!
Ah, you mad Majnun! Lost, forever you've gone...
the world is full, full of love, but there's not a one;
no one who ever bowed down at Beauty's shrine,
had a soul devoid of sin like yours... O so very fine!

Summer is bright: Autumn, greenness fades away,
trees are a sickly colour, unnourished by the dew;
sap running from root and branch and leaf distils,
drying in chilly air, groves become bare like hills;
the garden's flowers winds disperse on every side:

all sight and smell loved... Autumn throws aside.
And so Layla's Summer hours have slowly passed,
now she feels the hurtful blow of Autumn's blast
with her bowers, her blooming bowers... assailed,
the perfume of the rose is gone, is finally exhaled;
withered leaves, burnt petals bestrew the ground,
nothing but desolation reigns everywhere around:
from the moment she saw Majnun's mental state
her heart had no peace, hope it couldn't cultivate.
But before the overwhelming misery came her way
thoughts of a new life lifted her heart each day...
in the middle of her bitterest weeping and distress,
in the middle of dark broodings of her loneliness...
though feelings crushed... and that man she loved
a forest wanderer... who with wild beasts roamed,
still there was hope, and still was her mental gaze
fixed upon the expected joys of forthcoming days.
But now... now all hope had perished! For she had
seen the workings of that noble mind... gone mad:
that delirious fit and then that appalling fleeing...
grief, terror seized her heart that began trembling.
She does not cry, but in deep despair pines away...

that blight is now on her fair face perhaps to stay,
worm has turned in... its destined prey has bound:
frightening symptoms of a swift decay are found
to have come over her fair form... that in the strife
she almost sinks away beneath the load of her life.
Now... feeling ebbing away her life's receding tide
she calls her poor, weeping mother to her bedside:
"Mother, my time's come, you don't need anymore
to complain... for my heart can't conceal anymore
what was once useless to reveal... and yet... now
in spite of love, you might blame my passion, now.
But in my rapture I've drunk poison in love's cup...
and feel agony searing soul, drying these tears up.
O mother, all I crave when I am lying in my grave
is that mad, faithful youth, whose truth that gave
our souls to be blended into one, may finally come
and... weep upon his faithful Layla's lonely tomb.
Don't stop him... let him pour forth all his despair,
and let none intrude on his sacred solitude, there:
for he to me is my life, my path, my truth, my way
and far more precious to me... as this light of day.
His love is an amazing love, a love that is sublime,

which has mocked the power of fate and of time...
when you finally see him in the dust, nearby here,
wildly shouting and crying, lamenting on my bier,
do not get upset... please kindly, soothingly relate
whatever you know about me, my disastrous fate.
Say to that woe-begotten wanderer... 'All is over;
Layla, your own sad friend, is no more... no more;
from this world's heavy chains she is forever free,
to you her heart was given, she died only for *thee!*
With love so perfectly blended was her life, so true
that other than love... no other joy she ever knew.
Not one worldly care her thoughts ever oppressed:
it was only her love for you that disturbed her rest,
and in that love of hers her gentle spirit passed...
breathing on you her love's blessing to the last.'"
That mournful mother gazed upon her dying child,
now silent... although her lips imploring, smiled;
saw the dreaded change, a sudden pause of breath,
she saw her beauty settle into the trance of death,
and, in the frenzy of her anguish and grief she tore
her grey hair, then an embroidered dress she wore;
dissolving into tears, her wild and sorrowing cries

brought down compassion from the weeping skies,
and so intense was her grief, she shivered, fell full
prostrate upon her daughter's corpse... insensible,
and never, never did she rise again, for the thread
of life was broken... both, clasped together... dead!

O treacherous world of angelic form, devil's heart;
rosary beads in hand... hiding a sharp killing dart.
The heavens are open with a welcome azure glow,
but the raging storms overwhelm our hopes below;
the ship is tossed by waves to crash on the shore,
the wanderer now will meet his friends no more...
upon a field of blooming flowers, or under a wave,
in both of them can be discovered a gaping grave...
because without any form... riding through the air,
death devouring everything is always everywhere;
Kai Khosrau and Kai-Kobad and even mighty Jam,
all in the end had to descended into a cold tomb...
tell, who is the one who is made from mortal clay,
that from the doom coming to all... can get away?
For this... in vain have youth and those of old age
looked for a solution in learning's mystical page...

no human power has as yet been able to penetrate
the answer to the mystery of this ever-ruling fate:
frail life's really relying on but a moment's breath,
ah no, it's true that this old world... is full of death.

How many wept for that fair one gone O so soon!
How many there wept... over that departed moon!
How many mourned... with a broken heart for her!
And how many bathed with tears... her sepulchre!
Around her pure dust, assembled old and young...
and upon the ground their fragrant offerings flung:
hallowed spot now, where loving youth and maid
time after time their homage out of respect, paid.
And once again it was the task of faithful Zayd,
though far-extending plains, across forests wide,
to seek out that man of many woes... and to tell
him the tragic fate of her... that he loved so well.
Loved and doted on, until his mind, overwrought,
was crushed under weight of intolerable thought.
With bleeding heart Zayd found his lonely abode,
watering with tears the path on which he had rode,
and... beating his sad breast, Majnun perceived

his friend's approach, asked him why he grieved;
what withering sorrow upon his cheek had preyed,
and why in a melancholy black was he arrayed...
"O no," he cried, "hail has crushed all the bowers;
a sudden storm has blown away all of my flowers;
the cypress has crashed, its leaves are burnt away
and moon falling out of its orbit has lost the way!
Layla is *dead!*" No sooner was that dreaded word
uttered, no sooner were the terrible tidings heard,
than Majnun... as sudden as a lightning's stroke
sank onto the ground, unconscious from the shock,
and lay there not moving... for it was as if his life
had been snuffed out by the wind of mortal strife.
When he began to recover and he prepared to rise,
a re-awakened mad frenzy was glaring in his eyes:
then... as he staggered to his feet, a hollow groan
burst from his heart... "Now, ah, now I am *alone!*
O why have you these terrifying words expressed?
And, why have you plunged a dagger in my chest?
Away, go away, away!" The savage beasts around
him... in a wide circle they crouched on the ground
and wondering looked on... while furiously he rent

his tattered garments... and then his loud lament
rang through the echoing forest. Now... he treads
the mazes of that shadowy wood, which spreads
a perpetual gloom, and eventually emerges where
no bower and no grove obstructs that heated air;
he climbs to mountain's brow, over hill and plain
urged onwards more quickly by his burning brain,
hurrying across where desert's arid boundary lies:
and Zayd, like his shadow, follows where he flies;
and when the tomb of Layla comes into his view,
he falls and his tears drop to the ground like dew;
rolling... distraught, he spreads his arms to clasp
the sacred temple and writhes like an injured asp:
despair and horror swell out his ceaseless moan...
and still he holds like her that monumental stone.
"O no," he cries... "O no more shall I ever behold
that angel-face, that dear form of heaven's mould.
She was the rose that I cherished, but a mere gust
of sickening wind has quickly laid her in the dust.
She was my favourite cypress, full of sweet grace,
but death has snatched her from her resting-place.
That tyrant has deprived me of this perfect flower

that I had planted deep in my own secluded bower;
the sweet basil... choicest that has ever been seen,
so cruelly torn... and now scattered over the green.
O beautiful flower... nipped by that Winter's cold,
gone from this world you never really did behold.
O bower of joy... with blossoms so fresh and fair,
but doomed, ah no... no ripened fruit to ever bear.
Where shall I find you, now in darkness shrouded?
Those eyes of liquid light now are forever clouded!
Where are those carnation lips... that musky mole
upon your cheek... that treasure of heart and soul?
Though hidden from my eyes those charms so fine,
still they're blooming in this loving heart of mine:
although far removed from all that I held so dear,
although all I loved on earth is lying buried here,
remembrance of the past new enchantment gives:
memory, blessed memory... in heart she still lives.
Yes... although you have left this contentious life,
this scene of endless treachery and endless strife,
and... I like you shall soon all of my chains burst,
and quench in gulps of heavenly love, my thirst...
there where the angelic bliss can never end or cloy

and where we soon shall meet... in everlasting joy;

the lit candle of our souls... more clear and bright,

will be so lustrous... shining with immortal light!"

He ceased, and from that tomb to which he clung

suddenly off to some distance he wildly sprung...

and then seated upon his camel, he took the way

leading to there... where his father's mansion lay;

his troop of guards, servant-beasts, as usual near,

with still unchanged devotion... at front and rear,

yet, all unconscious of where recklessly he went...

to vent his passion he went... on no purpose bent,

he sped along, or stopped... the woods and plains

resounding with his poetry's melancholic strains:

poems of those that from one of broken spirit flow,

the wailing and sighing of his never-ending woe...

but, the same sudden frenzy which fired his mind

to strangely be leaving his Layla's grave behind...

now, drove him back, and with even greater grief,

sighing and weeping... and hopeless of any relief,

he throws himself down on the tomb once again,

as if he on that blessed spot forever will remain...

to mingle, as if dead, with her dead form beneath:

the young and the pure and the beautiful in death.
He held the marble even more closely to his chest,
and a thousand kisses eagerly upon it he pressed,
he knocked his forehead in such a desperate mood
all the marble around him was stained with blood.
Alone, unseen, his wild animal guards kept remote
any curious intruders coming to that sacred spot:
alone, with his wasted form and sad, somber eyes,
groaning with pain on her grave he exhausted lies
and no more of life's joys or miseries will he meet,
there's nothing to rouse him from this last retreat;
upon this sinking gravestone he has laid his head,
the gates... are already creaking open, for the dead!

Now Selim, the generous... who had twice before
sought out his refuge in the wilderness, to implore
the love-sick wanderer to renounce the life he led,
to shun the ruin that was bursting over his head,
once again explored that wilderness... once again
crossed craggy rock, deep valley and dusty plain
to find his new abode. A long month had passed
amongst the wilds... when, turning back, at last

he could see the wretched sufferer this time alone,
stretched upon the ground, his head upon a stone:
Majnun, suddenly looking up, recognized his face,
and told his growling followers to give him space,
then said... "Why are you here again... since you
left me angrily? What now do you wish me to do?
I am a wretch bowed down with the bitterest woe:
doomed, extremes of separation's misery to know,
while you, born into affluence, in pleasure nursed,
a stranger to tragedies... smallest and the worst,
can never be joining, unless in sickening mockery,
such a one who is lost to all of the world... as me!"
Selim replied: "Happily I would change your will,
and take you far away to be your companion still:
wealth shall be yours... peace and all society's joy,
days of tranquility... no suffering will you annoy;
and she... for whom your soul has yearned so long
may still be gained and none shall do you wrong!"
Deeply Majnun sighed, cried: "No more, no more!
Don't speak about the one whose memory I adore,
she whom I loved... held than life itself more dear,
my friend, my angel-bride, my love is buried here!

Dead! But her spirit is now in Paradise, while I...
live... and am dead from grief and yet I don't die.
This... is the fatal spot, my beloved Layla's tomb,
this... is the lamented place of love's martyrdom.
Here lies my life's sole treasure... life's sole trust;
all that was bright in beauty... now gone to dust!"
Selim before him in amazement, paralyzed, stood,
stricken with grief, began weeping tears of blood...
and then some consolation he sadly tried to give.
What consolation... can he make dear Layla live?
Those gentle words and sad looks were only found
to aggravate distraught Majnun's terrible wound,
and after weeks in fruitless sympathy had passed
and his patience still tried, he lingered to the last;
then, with an anxious heart and all hope had left,
that melancholic, tragic scene, reluctantly he left.
The life of Majnun had received the deadly blight,
his troubled day was closing fast, come the night.
He was still weeping... bitter, bitter tears he shed,
groveling in the dust... trembling hands he spread
out... then up in prayer: "God, your servant hear!
And in Your gracious Mercy, free him from here...

from all the afflictions which he must go through,
then in the Prophet's name he can return to You!"
Murmuring like this, on the tomb he laid his head,
and with an exhausted sigh... his weary spirit fled.

And Majnun too... has performed his pilgrimage.
And who ever that exists upon this earthly stage,
who follows the same path? Whatever his claim to
virtue, to honour, to worthy praise, or to blame;
whatsoever he'll answer at that judgment-throne,
where secrets are unveiled, and all things known;
where all deeds of deadly darkness meet the light,
and goodness wears its crown with a glory bright.
Majnun, now removed from this tumultuous scene
which had to him only an unceasing misery been...
at length slept... on the couch his bride possessed,
and on waking, saw her mingled with the blessed.
There, lay stretched out his body for many a day...
protected by his subjects... faithful beasts of prey;
whose presence filled with fear all coming around,
seeking to know where Majnun might be found...
listening... they heard low murmurs on the breeze,

now loud and mournful like the humming of bees;
they still supposed him to be seated in his place...
watched by those wild sentinels of a savage race.
A year had passed, and still their watch they kept,
as if their sovereign was not dead, but only slept;
some had been called away, and some had died...
at last the decayed body was by onlookers spied;
and when the truth had caught the wind of fame,
many old friends from every quarter quickly came:
weeping, they washed his bones, now pure white,
with ceaseless tears all performed the funeral rite,
and... opening the tear-washed gravestone wide,
mournfully... laid him by his beloved Layla's side.
One promise bound their faithful hearts... one bed
of cold earth united them... when they were dead.
Separated in their short life, how cruel their doom!
Never to be joined alive... only in the silent tomb!

The Arabian minstrels legendary songs chronicle
the young lovers tragedy and also delight to dwell
upon their matchless purity... their undying faith,
and how their dust was united, together in death:

it's told... Zayd saw in a dream the radiant bride
Layla with a blissful Majnun, seated side by side.
Zayd one night, dreaming, flashed into his sight...
stretching before him... endless vistas of delight
and experiencing the world of spirits... as he lay,
many glowing angels appeared and there did stay
with many circles of glory around them gleaming,
their eyes with holy rapture towards him beaming
and as he gazed he saw the ever-verdant bowers..
with golden fruit glowing... and blooming flowers;
the nightingales he heard: their sweetness among
their warbling of their rich and melodious song...
and the ring-dove's murmuring and then the swell
of the melody from the harp and the conch shell...
and then... he saw standing in a rose-laden glade,
beneath a wavering palm-tree's extensive shade...
a throne... a throne that was amazing to behold,
all studded with glittering gems, made of gold...
and gorgeous celestial carpets near it were spread,
close to where pure water ran along a river's bed;
and there upon that throne, in their blissful state,
the long-parted lovers... in peaceful love did wait:

resplendent, they sat there in that heavenly light,
and their hands held a cap with diamonds bright;
their lips in turn... his, then hers with nectar wet,
in pure ambrosial kisses met, then met, then met...
sometimes, to the other their thoughts revealing...
each clasping the other with a most tender feeling.
Then... the dreamer who this glorious vision saw,
demanded, with an ever-increasing blinding awe,
what the sacred names were that this happy pair
in this glade of Iram were destined to forever bear.
A voice suddenly replied... "That sparkling moon
is still Layla and her friend is still called Majnun;
as they were deprived in your frail world, of bliss,
they are now reaping their great reward... in this!"
Then Zayd, on waking from his wondrous dream,
thought deeply and long upon its mystical theme,
and later he told to all how those faithful to love
will one day be recompensed by the highest Love.

All of you, who thoughtlessly continue to suppose
that all with worth this flattering world bestows,
reflect today upon just how transient is your stay

here... and how soon even the sorrows fade away!
Ah, the terrible pangs of grief the heart may wring
in life, but Paradise will finally remove the sting...
the world that comes... your happiness will secure
because that world to come is eternal, and is pure.
Ah... what other solace is there for the human soul
but a lasting peace... pure love's unchanging goal!

Winebringer! Now Nizami's poem is finally sung:
this Persian poet's pearls are in the circle strung...
and so, please fill once again this wine goblet high,
and, would you never be asking this imbiber why?
Fill this cup to that love that never changes, never!
Fill this cup to the love that goes on living forever!
To the love that has been purified by earthly woes
and at last with everlasting bliss... divinely glows!

MOST 6" x 9" (15 cm x 23 cm) PAPERBACKS PERFECTBOUND...
Most also available in pdf format
Cheapest from: www.newhumanitybooksbookheaven.com
check out our website for prices & full descriptions of each book.

TRANSLATIONS

[NOTE: All translations by Paul Smith are in clear, modern English and in the correct rhyme-structure of the originals and as close to the true meaning as possible.]

DIVAN OF HAFIZ
Revised Translation & Introduction by Paul Smith
This is a completely revised one volume edition of the only modern, poetic version of Hafiz's masterpiece of 791 *ghazals, masnavis, rubais* and other poems/songs. The spiritual and historical and human content is here in understandable, beautiful poetry: the correct rhyme-structure has been achieved, without intruding, in readable (and singable) English. In the Introduction of 70 pages his life story is told in greater detail than any where else; his spirituality is explored, his influence on the life, poetry and art of the East and the West, the form and function of his poetry, and the use of his book as a worldly guide and spiritual oracle. His Book, like the *I Ching,* is one of the world's Great Oracles. Included are notes to most poems, glossary and selected bibliography and two indexes. First published in a two-volume hardback limited edition in 1986 the book quickly went out of print. 542 pages.

PERSIAN AND HAFIZ SCHOLARS AND ACADEMICS WHO HAVE COMMENTED ON PAUL SMITH'S FIRST VERSION OF HAFIZ'S 'DIVAN'.
"It is not a joke... the English version of ALL the *ghazals* of Hafiz is a great feat and of paramount importance. I am astonished. If he comes to Iran I will kiss the fingertips that wrote such a masterpiece inspired by the Creator of all and I will lay down my head at his feet out of respect."
Dr. Mir Mohammad Taghavi (Dr. of Literature) Tehran.
"I have never seen such a good translation and I would like to write a book in Farsi and introduce his Introduction to Iranians." Mr B. Khorramshai, Academy of Philosophy, Tehran.
"Superb translations. 99% Hafiz 1% Paul Smith."Ali Akbar Shapurzman, translator of many mystical works in English to Persian and knower of Hafiz's *Divan* off by heart.
"I was very impressed with the beauty of these books." Dr. R.K. Barz. Faculty of Asian Studies, Australian National University.
"Smith has probably put together the greatest collection of literary facts and history concerning Hafiz." Daniel Ladinsky (Penguin Books author of poems inspired by Hafiz).

HAFIZ – THE ORACLE
(For Lovers, Seekers, Pilgrims, and the God-Intoxicated).
Translation & Introduction by Paul Smith. 441 pages.

HAFIZ OF SHIRAZ.
The Life, Poetry and Times of the Immortal Persian Poet.
In Three Books by Paul Smith. Over 1900 pages, 3 volumes.

PIERCING PEARLS: THE COMPLETE ANTHOLOGY OF PERSIAN POETRY
(Court, Sufi, Dervish, Satirical, Ribald, Prison & Social Poetry from the 9th to the 20th century.) Volume One
Translations, Introduction and Notes by Paul Smith. Pages 528.

PIERCING PEARLS: THE COMPLETE ANTHOLOGY OF PERSIAN POETRY
(Court, Sufi, Dervish, Satirical, Ribald, Prison & Social Poetry from the 9th to the 20th century.) Vol. Two
Translations, Introduction and Notes by Paul Smith. Pages 462.

DIVAN OF SADI: His Mystical Love-Poetry.
Translation & Introduction by Paul Smith. 421 pages.

RUBA'IYAT OF SADI
Translation & Introduction by Paul Smith. 151 pages.

WINE, BLOOD & ROSES: ANTHOLOGY OF TURKISH POETS
Sufi, Dervish, Divan, Court & Folk Poetry from the 14th – 20th Century
Translations, Introductions, Notes etc., by Paul Smith. Pages 286.

OBEYD ZAKANI: THE DERVISH JOKER.
A Selection of his Poetry, Prose, Satire, Jokes and Ribaldry.
Translation & Introduction by Paul Smith. 305 pages.

OBEYD ZAKANI'S > MOUSE & CAT ^ ^ (The Ultimate Edition) Translation & Introduction etc by Paul Smith. 191 pages.

THE GHAZAL: A WORLD ANTHOLOGY
Translations, Introductions, Notes, Etc. by Paul Smith. Pages 658.

NIZAMI: THE TREASURY OF MYSTERIES
Translation & Introduction by Paul Smith. 251 pages.

NIZAMI: LAYLA AND MAJNUN
Translation & Introduction by Paul Smith. 215 pages.

UNITY IN DIVERSITY
Anthology of Sufi and Dervish Poets of the Indian Sub-Continent
Translations, Introductions, Notes, Etc. by Paul Smith. Pages... 356.

RUBA'IYAT OF RUMI
Translation & Introduction and Notes by Paul Smith. 367 pages.

THE *MASNAVI*: A WORLD ANTHOLOGY
Translations, Introduction and Notes by Paul Smith. 498 pages.

HAFIZ'S FRIEND, JAHAN KHATUN: The Persian Princess Dervish Poet...
A Selection of Poems from her *Divan*
Translated by Paul Smith with Rezvaneh Pashai. 267 pages.

PRINCESSES, SUFIS, DERVISHES, MARTYRS & FEMINISTS:
NINE GREAT WOMEN POETS OF THE EAST:
A Selection of the Poetry of Rabi'a of Basra, Rabi'a of Balkh, Mahsati, Lalla Ded, Jahan Khatun, Makhfi, Tahirah, Hayati and Parvin.
Translation & Introduction by Paul Smith. Pages 367.

RUMI: SELECTED POEMS
Translation, Introduction & Notes by Paul Smith. 220 pages.

KABIR: SEVEN HUNDRED SAYINGS *(SAKHIS)*.
Translation & Introduction by Paul Smith. 190 pages. Third Edition

SHAH LATIF: SELECTED POEMS
Translation & Introduction by Paul Smith. 172 pages

LALLA DED: SELECTED POEMS
Translation & Introduction by Paul Smith. 140 pages.

BULLEH SHAH: SELECTED POEMS
Translation & Introduction by Paul Smith. 141 pages.

NIZAMI: MAXIMS
Translation & Introduction Paul Smith. 214 pages.

KHIDR IN SUFI POETRY: A SELECTION
Translation & Introduction by Paul Smith. 267 pages.

ADAM: THE FIRST PERFECT MASTER AND POET
by Paul Smith. 222 pages.

MODERN SUFI POETRY: A SELECTION
Translations & Introduction by Paul Smith. Pages 249

LIFE, TIMES & POETRY OF NIZAMI
by Paul Smith. 97 pages.

RABI'A OF BASRA: SELECTED POEMS
Translation by Paul Smith. 102 pages.

RABI'A OF BASRA & MANSUR HALLAJ
~Selected Poems~ Translation & Introduction Paul Smith. Pages 134

SATIRICAL PROSE OF OBEYD ZAKANI
Translation and Introduction by Paul Smith. 212 pages.

KHAQANI: SELECTED POEMS
Translation & Introduction by Paul Smith. 197 pages.

IBN 'ARABI: SELECTED POEMS
Translation & Introduction by Paul Smith. 121 pages.

THE *GHAZAL IN SUFI* & DERVISH POETRY: An Anthology:
Translations, Introductions, by Paul Smith Pages 548.

A GREAT TREASURY OF POEMS
BY GOD-REALIZED & GOD-INTOXICATED POETS
Translation & Introduction by Paul Smith. Pages 804.

MAKHFI: THE PRINCESS SUFI POET ZEB-UN-NISSA
A Selection of Poems from her *Divan*
Translation & Introduction by Paul Smith. 154 pages.

~ THE SUFI RUBA'IYAT ~
A Treasury of Sufi and Dervish Poetry in the *Ruba'i* form,
from Rudaki to the 21st Century
Translations, Introductions, by Paul Smith. Pages… 304.

LOVE'S AGONY & BLISS: ANTHOLOGY OF URDU POETRY
Sufi, Dervish, Court and Social Poetry from the 16th- 20th Century
Translations, Introductions, Etc. by Paul Smith. Pages 298.

RUBA'IYAT OF ANSARI
Translation & Introduction by Paul Smith. 183 pages

THE RUBAI'YAT: A WORLD ANTHOLOGY
Court, Sufi, Dervish, Satirical, Ribald, Prison and Social Poetry in the Ruba'i form from the
9th to the 20th century from the Arabic, Persian, Turkish, Urdu and English.
Translations, Introduction and Notes by Paul Smith Pages 388.

BREEZES OF TRUTH
Selected Early & Classical Arabic Sufi Poetry
Translations, Introductions by Paul Smith. Pages 248.

THE~DIVINE~WINE: A Treasury of Sufi and Dervish Poetry
(Volume One) Translations, Introductions by Paul Smith. Pages... 522.

THE~DIVINE~WINE: A Treasury of Sufi and Dervish Poetry
(Volume Two) Translations, Introductions by Paul Smith. Pages... 533.

TONGUES ON FIRE: An Anthology of the Sufi, Dervish,
Warrior & Court Poetry of Afghanistan.
Translations, Introductions, Etc. by Paul Smith. 322 pages.

THE SEVEN GOLDEN ODES (QASIDAS) OF ARABIA
(The Mu'allaqat)
Translations, Introduction & Notes by Paul Smith. Pages... 147.

THE QASIDA: A WORLD ANTHOLOGY
Translations, Introduction & Notes by Paul Smith. Pages... 354.

IBN AL-FARID: WINE & THE MYSTIC'S PROGRESS
Translation, Introduction & Notes by Paul Smith. 174 pages.

RUBA'IYAT OF ABU SA'ID
Translation, Introduction & Notes by Paul Smith. 227 pages.

RUBA'IYAT OF BABA TAHIR
Translations, Introduction & Notes by Paul Smith. 154 pages.

THE POETS OF SHIRAZ
Sufi, Dervish, Court & Satirical Poets from the 9th to the 20th
Centuries of the fabled city of Shiraz .
Translations & Introduction & Notes by Paul Smith. 428 pages.

RUBA'IYAT OF 'ATTAR
Translation, Introduction & Notes by Paul Smith. 138 Pages.

RUBA'IYAT OF MAHSATI
Translation, Introduction & Notes by Paul Smith. 150 Pages.

RUBA'IYAT OF JAHAN KHATUN
Translation by Paul Smith with Rezvaneh Pashai
Introduction & Notes by Paul Smith. 157 Pages.

RUBA'IYAT OF SANA'I
Translation, Introduction & Notes by Paul Smith. 129 Pages.

RUBA'IYAT OF JAMI
Translation, Introduction & Notes by Paul Smith. 179 Pages.

RUBA'IYAT OF SARMAD
Translation, Introduction & Notes by Paul Smith. 381 pages.

RUBA'IYAT OF HAFIZ
Translation, Introduction & Notes by Paul Smith. 221 Pages.

GREAT SUFI POETS OF THE PUNJAB & SINDH:
AN ANTHOLOGY
Translations & Introductions by Paul Smith 166 pages.

YUNUS EMRE, THE TURKISH DERVISH:
SELECTED POEMS
Translation, Introduction & Notes by Paul Smith. Pages 237.

RUBA'IYAT OF KAMAL AD-DIN
Translation, Introduction & Notes by Paul Smith. Pages 170.

RUBA'YAT OF KHAYYAM
Translation, Introduction & Notes by Paul Smith
Reprint of 1909 Introduction by R.A. Nicholson. 268 pages.

RUBA'IYAT OF AUHAD UD-DIN
Translation and Introduction by Paul Smith. 127 pages.

RUBA'IYAT OF AL-MA'ARRI
Translation & Introduction by Paul Smith. 151 pages

ANTHOLOGY OF CLASSICAL ARABIC POETRY
(From Pre-Islamic Times to Al-Shushtari)
Translations, Introduction and Notes by Paul Smith. Pages 287.

THE *QIT'A*
Anthology of the 'Fragment' in Arabic, Persian and Eastern Poetry.
Translations, Introduction and Notes by Paul Smith. Pages 423.

HEARTS WITH WINGS
Anthology of Persian Sufi and Dervish Poetry
Translations, Introductions, Etc., by Paul Smith. Pages 623.

HAFIZ: SELECTED POEMS
Translation, Introduction & Notes by Paul Smith. 227 Pages.

'ATTAR: SELECTED POETRY
Translation, Introduction & Notes by Paul Smith. 222 pages.

SANA'I : SELECTED POEMS
Translation, Introduction & Notes by Paul Smith. 148 Pages.

THE ROSE GARDEN OF MYSTERY: SHABISTARI
Translation by Paul Smith.
Introduction by E.H. Whinfield & Paul Smith. Pages 182.

RUDAKI: SELECTED POEMS
Translation, Introduction & Notes by Paul Smith. 142 pages.

SADI: SELECTED POEMS
Translation, Introduction & Notes by Paul Smith. 207 pages.

JAMI: SELECTED POEMS
Translation, Introduction by Paul Smith. 183 Pages.

NIZAMI: SELECTED POEMS
Translation & Introduction by Paul Smith. 235 pages.

RUBA'IYAT OF BEDIL
Translation & Introduction by Paul Smith. 154 pages.

BEDIL: SELECTED POEMS
Translation & Introduction by Paul Smith. Pages… 147.

ANVARI: SELECTED POEMS
Translation & Introduction by Paul Smith. 164 pages.

RUBA'IYAT OF 'IRAQI
Translation & Introduction by Paul Smith. 138 pages.

THE WISDOM OF IBN YAMIN: SELECTED POEMS
Translation & Introduction Paul Smith. 155 pages.

NESIMI: SELECTED POEMS
Translation & Introduction by Paul Smith. 169 pages.

SHAH NI'TMATULLAH: SELECTED POEMS
Translation & Introduction by Paul Smith. 168 pages.

AMIR KHUSRAU: SELECTED POEMS
Translation & Introduction by Paul Smith. 201 pages.

A WEALTH OF POETS:
Persian Poetry at the Courts of Sultan Mahmud in Ghazneh
& Sultan Sanjar in Ganjeh (998-1158)
Translations, Introduction and Notes by Paul Smith. Pages 264.

SHIMMERING JEWELS: Anthology of Poetry Under the Reigns
of the Mughal Emperors of India (1526-1857)
Translations, Introductions, Etc. by Paul Smith. Pages 463.

RAHMAN BABA: SELECTED POEMS
Translation & Introduction by Paul Smith. 141 pages.

RUBA'IYAT OF DARA SHIKOH
Translation & Introduction by Paul Smith. 148 pages.

ANTHOLOGY OF POETRY OF THE CHISHTI SUFI ORDER
Translations & Introduction by Paul Smith. Pages 313.

POEMS OF MAJNUN
Translation & Introduction by Paul Smith. 220 pages.

RUBA'IYAT OF SHAH NI'MATULLAH
Translation & Introduction by Paul Smith. 125 pages.

ANSARI: SELECTED POEMS
Translation & Introduction by Paul Smith. 156 pages.

BABA FARID: SELECTED POEMS
Translation & Introduction by Paul Smith. 164 pages.

POETS OF THE NI'MATULLAH SUFI ORDER
Translations & Introduction by Paul Smith. 244 pages.

MU'IN UD-DIN CHISHTI: SELECTED POEMS
Translation & Introduction by Paul Smith. 171 pages.

QASIDAH BURDAH:
THE THREE POEMS OF THE PROPHET'S MANTLE
Translations & Introduction by Paul Smith. Pages 116.

KHUSHAL KHAN KHATTAK: THE GREAT POET
& WARRIOR OF AFGHANISTAN, SELECTED POEMS
Translation & Introduction by Paul Smith. Pages 187.

RUBA'IYAT OF ANVARI
Translation & Introduction by Paul Smith. 104 pages.

'IRAQI: SELECTED POEMS
Translation & Introduction by Paul Smith. 156 pages.

MANSUR HALLAJ: SELECTED POEMS
Translation & Introduction by Paul Smith. Pages 178.

RUBA'IYAT OF BABA AFZAL
Translation & Introduction by Paul Smith. 178 pages.

RUMI: SELECTIONS FROM HIS *MASNAVI*
Translation & Introduction by Paul Smith. 260 pages.

WINE OF LOVE: AN ANTHOLOGY,
Wine in the Poetry of Arabia, Persia, Turkey & the Indian Sub-Continent
from Pre-Islamic Times to the Present
Translations & Introduction by Paul Smith. 645 pages.

GHALIB: SELECTED POEMS
Translation & Introduction by Paul Smith. Pages 200.

THE ENLIGHTENED SAYINGS OF HAZRAT 'ALI
The Right Hand of the Prophet
Translation & Introduction by Paul Smith. Pages 260.

HAFIZ: TONGUE OF THE HIDDEN
A Selection of *Ghazals* from his *Divan*
Translation & Introduction Paul Smith. 133 pages. Third Edition.

~ HAFIZ: A DAYBOOK ~
Translation & Introduction by Paul Smith. 375 pages.

~* RUMI* ~ A Daybook
Translation & Introduction by Paul Smith. Pages 383.

SUFI POETRY OF INDIA ~ A Daybook~
Translation & Introduction by Paul Smith. Pages 404.

~ SUFI POETRY~ A Daybook
Translation & Introduction by Paul Smith. Pages 390.

~*KABIR*~ A Daybook
Translation & Introduction by Paul Smith. 382 pages.

~ABU SA'ID & SARMAD~ A Sufi Daybook
Translation & Introduction by Paul Smith. 390 pages.

~ *SADI* ~ A Daybook
Translation & Introduction by Paul Smith. 394 pages.

NIZAMI, KHAYYAM & 'IRAQI ... A Daybook
Translation & Introduction by Paul Smith. 380 pages.

ARABIC & AFGHAN SUFI POETRY ... A Daybook
Translation & Introduction by Paul Smith. 392 pages.

TURKISH & URDU SUFI POETS... A Daybook
Translation & Introduction by Paul Smith. 394 pages.

SUFI & DERVISH RUBA'IYAT (9th – 14th century)
A DAYBOOK
Translation & Introduction by Paul Smith. 394 pages.

SUFI & DERVISH RUBA'IYAT (14thth – 20th century)
A DAYBOOK
Translation & Introduction by Paul Smith. 394 pages.

~SAYINGS OF THE BUDDHA: A DAYBOOK~
Revised Translation by Paul Smith from F. Max Muller's. 379 pages.

GREAT WOMEN MYSTICAL POETS OF THE EAST
~ A Daybook ~ Translation & Introduction by Paul Smit. 385 pages.

ABU NUWAS SELECTED POEMS
Translation & Introduction by Paul Smith. 154 pages.

HAFIZ: THE SUN OF SHIRAZ:
Essays, Talks, Projects on the Immortal Poet
by Paul Smith. 249 pages.

~ *NAZIR AKBARABADI* ~ SELECTED POEMS
Translation and Introduction Paul Smith. 191 pages.

* ~RUBA'IYAT OF IQBAL~ *
Translation & Introduction by Paul Smith. 175 pages.

~ *IQBAL* ~ SELECTED POETRY
Translation & Introduction by Paul Smith. 183 pages.

>THE POETRY OF INDIA<
Anthology of Poets of India from 3500 B.C. to the 20th century
Translations, Introductions... Paul Smith. Pages... 622.

BHAKTI POETRY OF INDIA... AN ANTHOLOGY
Translations & Introductions Paul Smith. Pages 236.

SAYINGS OF KRISHNA: A DAYBOOK
Translation & Introduction Paul Smith. Pages 376.

~CLASSIC POETRY OF AZERBAIJAN~ An Anthology~
Translation & Introduction Paul Smith. 231 pages.

THE TAWASIN: MANSUR HALLAJ
(Book of the Purity of the Glory of the One)
Translation & Introduction Paul Smith. Pages 264.

MOHAMMED In Arabic, Sufi & Eastern Poetry
Translation & Introduction by Paul Smith. Pages 245.

GITA GOVINDA
The Dance of Divine Love of Radha & Krishna
>Jayadeva< Translation by Puran Singh & Paul Smith. Pages 107.

GREAT WOMEN MYSTICAL POETS OF THE EAST
~ A Daybook ~ Translation & Introduction by Paul Smith. 385 pages.

~SUFI LOVE POETRY~ An Anthology
Translation & Introduction Paul Smith. Pages 560.

HUMA: SELECTED POEMS OF MEHER BABA
Translation & Introduction Paul Smith. Pages 244.

RIBALD POEMS OF THE SUFI POETS
Abu Nuwas, Sana'i, Anvari, Mahsati, Rumi, Sadi and Obeyd Zakani
Translation & Introduction Paul Smith. 206 pages.

FIVE GREAT EARLY SUFI MASTER POETS
Mansur Hallaj, Baba Tahir, Abu Sa'id, Ansari & Sana'i
SELECTED POEMS
Translation & Introduction by Paul Smith. Pages 617

FIVE GREAT CLASSIC SUFI MASTER POETS
Khaqani, Mu'in ud-din Chishti, 'Attar & Auhad ud-din Kermani
SELECTED POEMS
Translation & Introduction Paul Smith. Pages 541.

ANTHOLOGY OF WOMEN MYSTICAL POETS
OF THE MIDDLE-EAST & INDIA
Translation & Introduction Paul Smith. Pages 497.

ANTHOLOGY OF GREAT SUFI & MYSTICAL POETS OF PAKISTAN
Translation & Introduction by Paul Smith. Pages 260.

ZARATHUSHTRA: SELECTED POEMS
A New Verse Translation and Introduction by Paul Smith
from the Original Translation by D.J. Irani.
Original Introduction by Rabindranath Tagore. 141 pages.

THE DHAMMAPADA: The Gospel of the Buddha
Revised Version by Paul Smith
from translation from the Pali of F. Max Muller. 247 pages

THE YOGA SUTRAS OF PATANJALI
"The Book of the Spiritual Man" An Interpretation By Charles Johnston, General
Introduction by Paul Smith. Pages 173.

BHAGAVAD GITA: The Gospel of the Lord Shri Krishna
Translated from Sanskrit with Introduction by Shri Purohit Swami,
General Introductions by Charles Johnston Revised into Modern English
with an Introduction by Paul Smith. 326 pages.

~TAO TE CHING~ by Lao Tzu
Modern English Version by Paul Smith
from the Translation from the Chinese by Paul Carus. Pages 147.

THE PERSIAN ORACLE: Hafiz of Shiraz
Translation, Introduction & Interpretations by Paul Smith
Pages 441.

CAT & MOUSE: Obeyd Zakani
Translation & Introduction by Paul Smith
7" x 10" Illustrated 183 pages

HAFEZ: THE DIVAN
Volume One: The Poems
Revised Translation Paul Smith
"7 x 10" 578 pages.

HAFEZ: THE DIVAN
Volume Two: Introduction
Paul Smith 7" x 10" 224 pages.

~ SAADI ~ THE DIVAN
Revised Translation & Introduction Paul Smith
7" x 10" 548 pages.

~Introduction to Sufi Poets Series~

Life & Poems of the following Sufi poets, Translations & Introductions: Paul Smith

AMIR KHUSRAU, ANSARI, ANVARI, AL-MA'ARRI, 'ATTAR, ABU SA'ID, AUHAD UD-DIN, BABA FARID, BABA AZFAL, BABA TAHIR, BEDIL, BULLEH SHAH, DARA SHIKOH, GHALIB, HAFIZ, IBN 'ARABI, IBN YAMIN, IBN AL-FARID, IQBAL, INAYAT KHAN, 'IRAQI, JAHAN KHATUN, JAMI, KAMAL AD-DIN, KABIR, KHAQANI, KHAYYAM, LALLA DED, MAKHFI, MANSUR HALLAJ, MU'IN UD-DIN CHISHTI, NAZIR AKBARABADI, NESIMI, NIZAMI, OBEYD ZAKANI, RAHMAN BABA, RUMI, SANA'I, SADI, SARMAD, SHABISTARI, SHAH LATIF, SHAH NI'MAT'ULLAH, SULTAN BAHU, YUNUS EMRE, EARLY ARABIC SUFI POETS, EARLY PERSIAN SUFI POETS, URDU SUFI POETS, TURKISH SUFI POETS, AFGHAN SUFI POETS 90 pages each.

POETRY

THE MASTER, THE MUSE & THE POET
An Autobiography in Poetry by Paul Smith. 654 Pages.

~A BIRD IN HIS HAND~
POEMS FOR AVATAR MEHER BABA
by Paul Smith. 424 pages.

PUNE: THE CITY OF GOD (A Spiritual Guidebook to the New Bethlehem)
Poems & Photographs in Praise of Avatar Meher Baba
by Paul Smith. 159 pages.

COMPASSIONATE ROSE
Recent *Ghazals* for Avatar Meher Baba by Paul Smith. 88 pages.

~THE ULTIMATE PIRATE~ (and the Shanghai of Imagination)
A FABLE by Paul Smith. 157 pages.

+THE CROSS OF GOD+ A Poem in the *Masnavi* Form
by Paul Smith (7 x 10 inches).

···RUBA'IYAT ~ of ~ PAUL SMITH··· Pages 236.

SONG OF SHINING WONDER
& OTHER *MASNAVI* POEMS
Paul Smith. Pages 171.

~TEAMAKER'S *DIVAN... GHAZALS*~
Paul Smith. Pages 390.

CRADLE MOUNTAIN
Paul Smith... Illustrations – John Adam. (7x10 inches) Second Edition.

~BELOVED & LOVER~
Ghazals by Paul Smith... inspired by Meher Baba Pages 410.

POEMS INSPIRED BY 'GOD SPEAKS' BY MEHER BABA
Paul Smith... Pages 168.

MEHER BABA'S SECLUSION HILL
Poems & Photographs by Paul Smith "7 x 10" 120 pages.

FICTION

THE FIRST MYSTERY A Novel of the Road...
by Paul Smith. 541 pages.

~THE HEALER AND THE EMPEROR~
A Historical Novel Based on a True Story
by Paul Smith Pages 149.

>>>GOING<<<BACK...
A Novel by Paul Smith. 164 pages.

THE GREATEST GAME
A Romantic Comedy Adventure With A Kick!
by Paul Smith 187 pages.

GOLF IS MURDER!
A Miles Driver Golfing Mystery
by Paul Smith. 176 pages.

THE ZEN-GOLF MURDER!
A Miles Driver Golfing Mystery
by Paul Smith 146 pages.

~RIANA~ A Novel
by Paul Smith 154 pages.

CHILDREN'S FICTION

PAN OF THE NEVER-NEVER
by Paul Smith 167 pages.

~HAFIZ~
The Ugly Little Boy who became a Great Poet
by Paul Smith 195 pages.

SCREENPLAYS

>>>GOING<<<BACK...
A Movie of War & Peace Based on a True Story ...
Screenplay by Paul Smith

HAFIZ OF SHIRAZ
The Life, Poetry and Times of the Immortal Persian Poet.
A Screenplay by Paul Smith

LAYLA & MAJNUN BY NIZAMI
A Screenplay by Paul Smith

PAN OF THE NEVER-NEVER ...
A Screenplay by Paul Smith

THE GREATEST GAME
A Romantic Comedy Adventure With A Kick!
A Screenplay by Paul Smith

GOLF IS MURDER!
Screenplay by Paul Smith

THE HEALER & THE EMPEROR
A True Story... Screenplay
by Paul Smith

THE * KISS ...
A Screen-Play by Paul Smith

THE ZEN-GOLF MURDER!
A Screenplay by Paul Smith

TELEVISION

HAFIZ OF SHIRAZ:
A Television Series
by Paul Smith

THE FIRST MYSTERY
A Television Series For The New Humanity
by Paul Smith
THE MARK: The Australian Game
A Thirteen-Part Doco-Drama for Television   by Paul Smith

PLAYS, MUSICALS

HAFIZ: THE MUSICAL DRAMA by Paul Smith

THE SINGER OF SHIRAZ
A Radio Musical-Drama on the Life of Persia's Immortal Poet,
Hafiz of Shiraz by Paul Smith

ART

MY DOGS
From the Sketchbooks of Gus Cohen. 8" x 10" 224 pages

A BRIDGE TO THE MASTER ... MEHER BABA
Paintings & Drawings, Poems & Essays by Oswald Hall
Edited & Introduction by Paul Smith 8" x 10" 337 pages.

MY VIEW
From the Sketchbooks of Gus Cohen, Barkers Creek Castlemaine
8" x 10" 210 pages.

KARL GALLAGHER: PAINTINGS & POETRY 150 pages.

"To penetrate into the essence of all being and significance
and to release the fragrance of that inner attainment
for the guidance and benefit of others, by expressing
in the world of forms, truth, love, purity and beauty...
this is the only game which has any intrinsic and absolute
worth. All other, happenings, incidents and attainments can,
in themselves, have no lasting importance."
Meher Baba